A FLYING GERBIL AND THE DRUNK GUY'S CLUB

A FLYING GERBIL

AND THE

DRUNK GUY'S CLUB

CPR for the Living
Word of God

TODD SLECHTA

LUMINARE PRESS
WWW.LUMINAREPRESS.COM

Luminare Press
442 Charnelton St.
Eugene, OR 97401
www.luminarepress.com

LCCN: 2020914316
ISBN: 978-1-64388-416-5

Dedicated to my older brother Dale,
who lost his fight with cancer.

CONTENTS

CHAPTER 1

What I Learned from Flying Gerbils

When I was growing up, my family had a variety of pets. We owned a couple of dogs: Pebbles the Boston Terrier and Missy, a mutt that was included "at no extra cost" with the house we purchased from family friends. For a short time, we also had a parakeet named Buddy, but quickly realized it didn't make sense to let a bird leave drops of excitement on our furniture when there were so many more desirable options outside.

I remember the day my father gathered the family to share the heartbreaking news that Buddy had somehow escaped, and how we should not be sad because he had returned to the wild from where he came (which, as I recall was the "wild" of Angelo's Pet Shop on 34th St.). And of course, being in Chicago, we also had rodents—but the ones we considered pets were two gerbils named Chip and Dale who, to my knowledge, never once danced suggestively for anyone.

The idea behind family pets is fundamentally sound: an opportunity to teach children how to care for living things without neglecting or killing them (a skill I desire my children to possess when I eventually move into their base-ment). Some even say that having pets adds a therapeutic element to life and that there is something healthy—even spiritual—in caring for a living thing whose desire is to simply be with you (the reason why cats are incapable of being therapeutic).

At the risk of sounding like a reminiscing old codger, my family didn't have much money when growing up, so we had to make do with what we had. We didn't have an Xbox (or an A through R Box for that matter), DVDs (VHS or Beta?) or the internet. Creativity was essential for my childhood entertainment and on this particularly muggy, Chicago summer day, all of my creative juices were laser-focused on a single feat.

I had been vigorously playing in the yard defending our home from imaginary, marauding pirates, when I decided to meander into the much-cooler basement to momentarily escape the heat. As I was perusing through our family's hidden treasures, I stumbled across eight helium-filled bal-loons that had somehow followed us home from a traveling carnival just the night before. Why they had already been cast into the basement for all things ancient, I didn't know, but I grabbed hold of the bunch, took them outside, and diligently tied a stick to each balloon string so they wouldn't float away. Then, I leaned back against the tree and tried to figure out what to do with them.

Perhaps I should pause the story here to clarify that my mind doesn't operate in the same way as most. I know that I'm a little different and some would even say I'm a bit off. Others would say that I'm an odd duck (though I've never met a duck that I felt was glaringly odd because, a duck's a duck, right?). My mind has always pondered things most people would dismiss as frivolous, a waste of time, or a danger to innocent people. My mind likes to try to wrap itself around life conundrums like:

If you butter toast and drop it, it is certain to fall butter side down. We also know that if we throw a cat in the air (so a "friend" told me), it is certain to land on its feet. What would happen if we duct-taped a piece of buttered toast on the back of a cat (butter side up of course since, this is science) and threw it into the air?

But I digress.

This summer morning, surrounded by eight helium balloons and a world of possibility, my neurons were in creative overdrive. After analyzing the possibilities, my gaze fell upon two empty milk cartons setting atop an overflowing garbage can in the ally. I walked over, pondered them for a moment, then with a growing sense that what I saw before me was nothing short of pure potential (perhaps the cure for cancer or a cleaner and cheaper alternative fuel), I grabbed them and headed toward our garage.

After digging around my father's tools, driven by some unseen force, I found an old, rusty saw and cut the tops off each carton. Feeling the momentum build as an idea began to emerge, I next grabbed an old nail and punched four tiny holes in the top of each corner of the remaining carton. I ran back to the tree to select four of the best helium balloons and then, careful not to accidentally lose them, I gently threaded the string of each balloon through one of the tiny holes and secured them with a sophisticated granny knot. Stepping back, chest bursting with pride, I gazed upon my creation: a miniature helium balloon, complete with a basket for the pilot!

Not one to rest on my laurels, I quickly moved to Phase II. Piling small rocks into the pilot basket and carefully letting go each time, I began to gauge how fast my balloon would gain or lose altitude. Following each test, I meticulously adjusted the rocks, playing with the gentle currents of the summer breeze. After I had mastered the aeronautical basics for miniature helium balloons, I grew restless for Phase III. All my miniature helium balloon needed now was a pilot! As I looked around, I noted my sister playing on the porch, but my mind quickly calculated that, even if she were still an infant and not six years-old, she simply was too much payload for the balloon. I needed someone smaller; someone…or some *thing* smaller; something like say…a gerbil!

Swept up in the intoxicating pursuit of unchartered boundaries, I raced into the house and roused one of our gerbils from his lazy slumber (I believe it was Chip), and whisked him to the launching pad near the tree. I lowered Chip gently into the basket but confess that, in my excitement and unbridled enthusiasm I failed to run the proper tests to be sure that the weight in the basket was enough to keep the balloon low to the ground. In a burst of youthful exuberance, I simply let go of the balloon at the precise moment a stronger-than-normal breeze pushed through our yard. It took but a fleeting moment to realize that the weight of Chip was not enough to maintain a low and, more importantly, recoverable orbit.

In seconds, the balloon had risen to approximately ten feet, beyond the reach of this 4'2" child, moving briskly along with the breeze, up over our chain link fence and into the neighbor's yard! In horror I watched as the balloon continued to rise, higher and higher, and, in short order, floated above the roof top of the two-story home five doors down! I could just make out Chip's tiny feet on the top edge of the basket as he peered over and, for a fleeting moment wondered what a gerbil would think when looking down from that height (It wouldn't make sense for them to think "Hey, those people are as small as gerbils.").

Snapping out of my philosophical state, I ran back to the garage, hopped onto my bike and tore off down the alley, watching anxiously as my test pilot continued to gain more altitude as he moved off toward the north. Because the neighborhood was set up in a grid system of city blocks, I couldn't ride my bike as the crow flies (or in this case, as the gerbil flies). With each turn, the balloon drifted further away and despite my feverish efforts to negotiate the grid, I could only watch helplessly as Chip kept floating higher and higher, drifting farther and farther, becoming tinier and tinier.

My mother had three rules when it came to playing in my neighborhood (I'm sure there were more, but three was all I could retain in any given moment): (1) don't take the dogs outside of the yard or they will run away, (2) don't do anything stupid and (3) stay on this side of the train tracks. Technically, I felt I had complied with at least two of the rules. Chip wasn't a dog, so the yard limitation didn't apply, and the exploration of flight is far from stupid. The train tracks, however, were a different matter since Chip's flight path was taking him beyond my established boundary.

Hoping against hope for a miracle, I pedaled onward as the railroad tracks drew closer with each passing second and, as they did, so also the point of no return, the moment of decision on whether to cross the tracks in defiance of my mother or simply let Chip go. Everything began to move in slow motion. I could clearly hear my heart beating, my exhausted breathing, the gravel of the road being churned beneath my tires, the baseball card flapping in the spokes and Chip's impassioned cry to save him (poetic license). With less than ten feet between me and the forbidden railroad tracks I took a deep breath and slammed on my breaks, skidding to a halt and fishtailing to a complete stop, parallel to the steel rails of the Burlington Northern. Chest heaving, all that remained for me to do was to watch the dust drift mockingly away in gentle pursuit of my doomed rodent pilot.

Defeated and helpless, I watched Chip float off to the north, gazing over the side of his milk carton basket. When he was finally out of sight, I sadly turned my bike toward home and began plotting how to blame the absence of one of our gerbils on the neighbor's cat. I never learned what happened to Chip. I like to think he landed in Tahiti, met a beautiful, female island gerbil and is living the good life in the warmth and sunshine of paradise (an appropriate reward for a brave rodent pioneer!). More likely, he got hung up on some power lines and became a surprise barbecue for some crows. In the end, I'm a realist.

Forty-five plus years later I still find myself on occasion remembering that day and thinking how different it could have ended had I known what I know now (for example, kite string tethering versus free flight!). In the wisdom of my current stage of life, I understand that new perspectives are, at first, always uncomfortable, but they do lead to growth and the possibility for a more healthy and successful future. Though I have no plans to fly another gerbil any time soon, future rodent pilots can rest assured that, if

I do, I've not grown comfortable and they will benefit from my new perspective.

THE BIBLE, AND PARTICULARLY THE NEW TESTAMENT, were written in the first century *after* the life and death of Jesus Christ. They were written by predominantly Jewish writers to a primarily Jewish audience and assumed that those who read them would be intimately aware of certain contextual details and nuances. The authors did not anticipate that, without those small, significant, contextual details, those of us reading the Bible 2,000+ years later would be at a disadvantage. This means it is likely that some of the Bible passages with which we are most comfortable are misunderstood and becoming aware of these details, though uncomfortable, will give us new, healthier perspectives on them. For those who truly desire to grow and who claim that the Bible has authority in their lives, this should be a welcome discomfort. As Canadian pastor and artist David Hayworth poignantly noted in one of his works of graffiti:[1]

THE BIBLE + YOUR INTERPRETATION =
YOUR INTERPRETATION

So, I offer what could be an uncomfortable perspective on what may have been—for many over their faith journey—familiar and comfortable Bible passages. Drawing from lessons, talks and sermons that, over the years, I have received as a student and shared as a pastor, teacher

---

1. Pastor Hayworth is not for the faint-of-heart. While I don't agree with everything he says, he is worth checking out at https://thelastingsupper.com/ or via social platforms @NakedPastor. You've been given fair warning.

or facilitator with various groups ranging from congregations to bible college classes to Christian and corporate retreats and conferences, I hope to cause a little healthy discomfort on the way to a more healthy biblical perspective and understanding. I believe anyone would agree that such health is desperately needed in the current church and culture crisis.

CHAPTER 2

What's in a Name?

(Genesis 32)

The name Jared is forever ruined for me. Jared was a 13-year-old that I met right out of seminary at one of the first churches I served. To be fair, Jared didn't irritate me the whole time. Just when I breathed—and that is probably because there are only two times in my life when I was left curled on the floor in the fetal position, whimpering for my mother. Both involved Jared. So it goes without saying that when my wife and I learned she was pregnant with our first child, we had already decided that, should this blessed child be a boy, the name Jared would not be a contender. Now, before you get all judgmental, rolling your eyes and muttering "Geez Todd. It's only a name." Let me ask you. How many kids do you know named Adolf, Atilla or Lucifer? I didn't think so!

Names are incredibly important, and I'm aware that my wife and I were not the first couple to anguish over what to name their children. There are so many considerations, ranging from family traditions and expectations (we successfully resisted pressure to name a potential son Oldrich) to the desire to be unique, but not ridiculous ("His name is pronounced 'Sam,' but the Q and second M are silent.") Expectant parents invest countless hours trying to imagine all the many ways the future name of their child could be twisted and/or rhymed in a disparaging way by all the horrible children they will face on the playground! It's why my parents didn't name me Richard, even though they liked it. There were simply too many variations and so they opted for the much safer choice of Todd (the second "d" is silent, not the "T," like Frank Simmons persuaded our whole third grade class to believe!).

THROUGHOUT SCRIPTURE, NAMES CARRIED AN OBVIOUS importance because people believed they carried powers that could have significant implications, not only for the individual who bore the name, but also for the surrounding culture in which he or she lived. In my studies, there appears to be three powers that the scripture consistently ascribes to names.

Most profoundly, **names have the power to create something**: in a sense bringing something fully into being and granting it the dignity of acknowledged existence. On a certain level, this makes sense because, in some ways, living things don't fully come into being until they have a name by which to be called. It would explain the subconscious dynamic that is at play when people work frantically to have a name selected *before* a child is born because, absent a name, a new life's basic element of dignity, a name by which to be acknowledged is, at the very least, delayed.

I had a close relative who waited for just over three weeks before giving a name to their newborn daughter Miranda! While we waited for a name, the extended family was forced to use an uncomfortable form of verbal gymnastics to try to come up with ways to refer to her ranging from the awkward "baby girl" to the comical "offspring-yet-to-be-named!" We laugh about it now, but without a specific name, for twenty-two days Miranda was, in a way, not afforded the full uniqueness and dignity of being human. On a profound level, her existence came to completion when we were able to look into her eyes, smile and say, "Hello Miranda" because, until then we were forced to use a definite article when we referred to her (*the* child or *the* baby) contrary to our innate and intense desire to vest her with the uniqueness and dignity afforded by a specific name.[2]

The ability to bring something into *full* existence, granting something the dignity of being completely acknowledged is a unique power that names afford. In a sense, giving something a name *completes* its creation.

Another power the scriptures appear to ascribe to names is **the power to set a destiny and trajectory to one's life or life circumstance.** For example, we named our youngest daughter Teryn and, to be perfectly transparent, we picked it because we thought it was unique, not too crazy and rolled off the tongue well when used in the context of her full name. Throughout Teryn's life my wife and I have lost track of the countless times people went out of their way to comment on how Teryn's innocent and endless joy make her stand out amidst her peers. Teachers, friends of Teryn, their parents, strangers in three countries, on two

---

2. As an aside, it is this dynamic that lies at the foundation of one of my pet peeves, namely when men refer to their spouse as *the* wife or *the* woman. While perhaps meant to be cute or endearing, it intimates that she is an object or serves a function rather than someone with whom a lifetime together was chosen, and the helpmate that God sees as the remedy to it not being good for man to be alone.

continents, in two languages and numerous people across cultures have never failed to mention how unique they find Teryn's personality to be, especially how brightly her vast reservoir of empathy and optimism shine. Though I may be biased, as her father I would say that Teryn is compellingly empathetic, optimistic and happy.

When Teryn was twelve, my wife and I decided to delve into the etymology of her name. It turns out that Teryn is a modern derivative of the name Tara. It seems that Tara was the geographical name of the mythological seat of the ancient Irish kings, coming from the Gaelic *tor*, meaning hill or mound, and from which we get the word tower. Tara eventually came to be associated with the cultural belief of a sacred hill near Dublin where Irish high kings and queens lived. Over time, and as words do, Tara eventually came to be utilized in common, everyday communication as a word that means unique or shining. For those who have had the privilege of knowing our daughter, shining and unique are more than appropriate words to describe her. In a sense, Teryn lived into the meaning of her name or, to phrase it another way that reflects this biblical power, by giving our daughter the name Teryn, we set her on a life trajectory into which she is now living, bringing a shining uniqueness to her relationships.

The setting of a destiny or trajectory for one's life or life circumstance is another unique power that scripture seems to afford to names.

Finally, ***utilizing a name to commemorate an event or declare a state of being is yet another power*** the scriptures seem to afford names, and is the reason behind the name of our oldest daughter, Kyssa (pronounced "k-eye-sah").

During my university years, I had opportunity to partic-ipate in an exchange program in Sweden, and that is when

I first encountered the name (in Swedish spelled Kajsa). We chose Kyssa's name in order to commemorate an event. Without going into too much detail, we almost lost Kyssa at birth, being premature, needing intubation and an initial, nail-biting time in a neonatal intensive care unit. The word for kiss in Swedish is "kyss" (pronounced "shiss") and in Swedish folklore, a kiss is something that is life-giving (sort of like Prince Charming's kiss of Snow White, minus the reality of how bad her breath must have been after such an extended slumber). We named our daughter Kyssa because we believe that God kissed her that day and our desire was to commemorate it through her name, remembering how God's divine kiss granted her life.

Using names to commemorate an event or declare a state of being is evidenced in scripture, especially if you were the child of an Old Testament prophet. It was not uncommon that these children were given names that reflected the essence of the prophecies their fathers were delivering regarding the spiritual state of the Kingdom of Israel. For example, Hosea's first daughter was named Lo Rumahah which means "not loved" (Hosea 1:6), declaring how God felt that Israel did not love him. His second son was named Lo Ammi which means "not my people" (Hosea 1:8), declaring God's feeling toward his rebellious chosen people. Not surprisingly, both of Hosea's children struggled with self-esteem.

Also, thanks to a tense moment between God and Moses, the scriptures also let us catch a glimpse into the name that God bestows upon himself. In Exodus 3:13-15 Moses discovers that God has *generously* given him an all-expense paid trip back to Egypt and, even though Moses is grateful for the opportunity (sarcasm intended), he is acutely aware that he is not the most popular man in Egypt. In fact, in Exodus 3:13 we see evidence of Moses' ready and willing heart as he shares with God a loophole that he believes gets him out of the assignment.

> *But Moses protested, "If I go to the people of Israel and tell them, 'The God of your ancestors has sent me to you,' they will ask me, 'What is his name?' Then what should I tell them?'" (NLT)*

Moses' hesitation is understandable. How smoothly would it go if he were to travel to Egypt and declare to the enslaved Hebrew people that he was sent by an entity without a name? So, God indulges Moses.

> *"I AM who I AM. Say this to the people of Israel: I AM has sent me to you." God also said to Moses, "Say this to the people of Israel: Yahweh, the God of your ancestors—the God of Abraham, the God of Isaac, and the God of Jacob—has sent me to you."*
>
> *This is my eternal name, my name to remember for all generations. (NLT, Exodus 3:14b-15)*

At first glance it feels like God is messing with Moses—but then there emerges a sophisticated simplicity and beauty in God's answer. In many ways, God's name for himself encompasses all three powers that the scriptures seem to ascribe to names. I AM is admittedly a strange name, but by bestowing it, the name does bring God into a slightly more accessible and fathomable existence for humans. In a sense, God more fully creates Himself to Moses through the name. Additionally, I AM does set a trajectory between God, Moses and the Hebrew people. It is a name into which they must live because, now that God *is*, He must now be engaged on some level, even if it is only to deny His existence. That God is *not*, is no longer an option and so the Hebrew people (and all humanity for that matter) are now on a trajectory that will forevermore encompass wrestling with the question of God's existence. To put it another way, God says to humans: I AM, and humans have only one of two fundamental responses: You is *or* You isn't![3]

For these reasons, I AM ultimately is declarative in nature: declaring that a relationship, whether engaged and cultivated or not, now exists between God and the Hebrew people. The only question before them now is, how good of a relationship will it be, because from God's perspective, the reality that it exists is incontrovertible, embodied in the inherent declaration of the name I AM. God's name contains a sophisticated simplicity and beauty that encompasses all three powers the scriptures seem to ascribe to names.

ARGUABLY THE FIRST RECORDED SASQUATCH SIGHTING is one of my favorite Old Testament stories. Found in Genesis 25 is a story of sibling peace and love (sarcasm intended) that begins with a woman named Rebekah giving birth to twins. Her first-bornw was a hairy, red baby with a face that only a mother could love. Rebekah and her husband Isaac, name their boy Esau which means hairy, a decision that, to this day, raises two critical questions. First, just how hairy was this baby, and second, how did they miss

---

3. Relax friend! I realize it is improper grammar. I was just trying to make a point.

the glaringly obvious name Harold? Shortly after Esau was born, his younger brother followed and the passage says, he was born grasping his older brother's hairy heel. Lacking creativity, Rebekah and Isaac name him Jacob which, not surprisingly means, grasps the heel. Interestingly, the phrase *grasps the heel* eventually emerges within the Hebrew culture as an idiom for deceives, or as some translations relate, *the deceiver.*

The two grow up and the eldest, Esau, becomes a sturdy, hunter-gatherer, a regular man of the land. Jacob on the other hand, becomes mommy's favorite, who apparently demonstrates a certain culinary flair for stews. One day Jacob is whipping up one of his award-winning recipes when Esau comes in from a day of hunting, gathering and wrestling a bear or two (think Gaston from *Beauty and the Beast*). Esau is understandably hungry *and* apparently prone to the melodramatic, because he feels that he is so hungry he is about to *die*! He demands that Jacob give him some of his stew and, though a bit of a momma's boy, Jacob possesses some business savvy because he agrees to give Esau some stew *in exchange* for Esau's firstborn birthright. In the culture of the time, significant benefits were bestowed upon the firstborn male in a family, especially after the father died. So, a birthright is important, and it seems that Esau recognized this because he spends about three seconds thinking it over before agreeing to Jacob's offer (he is, after all, about to die of hunger!).

Later, in Chapter 27 we learn that Isaac has grown old and is preparing to die. One of his dying wishes is that Esau hunt his favorite wild game and cook it for him the way he likes it. He tells Esau that, after he's enjoyed the meal, he will give Esau his blessing as the firstborn child, locking in all the benefits that come with that position. In the next room however, Isaac's wife Rebekah hears the exchange and springs into action, instructing her favorite child, Jacob, to bring her two young goats that she will prepare for Isaac, just the way he likes it. She goes on to share that her plan is to have Jacob go to Isaac and pretend to be Esau, deceiving Isaac into giving him the blessing instead.

Initially, this seems to be a poorly designed deception on many levels. Remember, Esau is hairy as a buffalo and Jacob comes across as more of a smooth-shaven male model! Not to worry though! Isaac has very poor eyesight which Rebekah—as mother and wife of the year— intends to exploit, because the passages relates that she takes the best clothes of Esau, puts them on Jacob and covers the smooth part of his hands and nape of his neck with hairy goatskins. Voila! Esau 2.0—and it works! After only a couple of scary moments, when it appears that Isaac is going to figure it out (27:22, 27), the deception works! Isaac is deceived into bestowing the firstborn blessing on Jacob!

When Esau discovers what Jacob has done, he is (mildly speaking) less than pleased, claiming in verse 36 that Jacob (which means *the deceiver*) had followed the trajectory and destiny set by his name. Then with all the subtlety of an angry Chicago mobster, Esau lets it be known that the moment his father dies, he's going to kill Jacob. Jacob is no fool and takes advantage of the window of opportunity to escape to a region of the country where he has a distant uncle named Laban (Chapter 29). While hiding out there, he falls in love with his cousin Rachel, and arranges with his uncle to marry her, agreeing to work seven years in a sort of early matrimony layaway program. Rachel, however, is not the oldest daughter of Laban, an honor that fell to Leah. So, after seven years of labor for his uncle, fulfilling the terms of the agreement, on the night that Jacob is to consecrate his marriage with Rachel, the Bible says Uncle Laban sneaked Leah into the bedroom and Jacob made love to her!

Imagine Jacob's surprise when, in the morning, he wakes up to find that he is officially married to Leah! When he asks his uncle why he deceived him, Uncle Laban answers that it is "…not our custom here to give the younger daughter in marriage before the older one…;" something Jacob suggests that, in the future might be better shared beforehand. Fortunately, Uncle Laban *generously* agrees to allow Jacob to marry Rachel only a week after his marriage to Leah in return for another short seven years of service. So, it all works out in the end, and all three of them live happily ever after, as Leah reveals in her tell-all book entitled *Confessions of a Third Wheel: The Leah Story.*

So, WHY IS ALL THIS BACKGROUND IMPORTANT AND what does it have to do with names?

Let's start by asking and answering these questions:

Who is the one acting deceptively when it comes to bargaining away a birthright that can only be bestowed by a father's blessing? Esau is the deceiver, because he knew the birthright couldn't be finalized without the blessing of his father, so of course it didn't take long for him to agree because he had nothing to lose.

Who is the one acting deceptively in the instance of securing Isaac's blessing for Jacob by deceiving Isaac? Rachel is the deceiver. Remember, she is the one who came up with the plan and helped implement it.

Who is the one acting deceptively in the instance where

Isaac ends up marrying two women? Uncle Laban is the deceiver, slipping Leah into the dark tent instead of Rachel.

So it begs the question, why is Jacob named the deceiver when it seems that everyone else is doing the deceiving? One of the powers that the scriptures appear to ascribe to names is that they are declarative in nature, revealing a state of existence. Could it be that the name Jacob is not a name of destiny, but rather a name that God uses to declare the relational state of deception that exists in this family, a family that is to become the basis of a whole new nation?

In fact, the lack of deception seems to be Jacob's DNA because he is even uncomfortably honest when he decides it's time to return home and face his brother, Esau. Jacob fully anticipates that Esau is still angry, so he devises a plan to bribe him with lots of gifts.

> For [Jacob] thought "I will pacify [Esau] with these gifts I am sending on ahead; later, when I see him, perhaps he will receive me." (NLT)

There is nothing deceptive there! Jacob's plan is to pacify his brother's anger with gifts. In other words, he plans to bribe his way back into good graces.

HERE'S WHERE IT GETS INTERESTING. THE BIBLE recounts that, as Jacob waits alone for morning to come, ushering in the day when he will encounter his brother for the first time in over fourteen years, "...a man wrestled with him until daybreak" (Genesis 32:24).

So many questions!

How did the man get into the camp?

Who started the wrestling match?

Was this a common practice, or was Jacob the victim of a lone-wolf, wrestling fanatic?

These questions notwithstanding, most interpretations of this passage agree that the man was an angel sent by God, or even God Himself who wrestled with Jacob. Figuratively or literally, the idea is that divinity in some way engaged Jacob in a wrestling match that night. Even more interestingly, Jacob apparently had some skill, because the passage goes on to say that he was winning the match! In other words, the divine was ready to tap out, probably because Jacob used the chicken wing, over-the-shoulder cross face (Google it). The passage says that Jacob had divinity in a sleeper hold and was refusing to release him until this divine agent blessed him.

But before blessing Jacob the deceiver, this divine agent establishes a new trajectory for Jacob's life by changing his name to Israel, meaning one who struggles or one who struggles with God and with humans (Genesis 32:28). Remember, one of the powers that scripture appears to ascribe to names is the ability to set a destiny for one's life. I would suggest that this is what is happening in this passage. Jacob, whose name to date has declared a state of relational deceptiveness in his family, is now called Struggles, and this becomes the destiny into which not only Rachel's son Jacob/Israel will live, but also the emerging Hebrew nation as well.

Wrap your head around what happens here! Before, Jacob is blessed, he is told by the angel as an agent of God that he will no longer live in a state of deception, self or otherwise, but rather live into a destiny of struggle!

How can a destiny marked by struggle be a good thing?

Because the opposite of caring is indifference. The opposite of caring is a disposition where one is so impervious to something or someone that there is no emotion, there is neither love, nor hate, only numb indifference.

Struggle indicates life and vitality. If I am honest with myself, I struggle constantly with those aspects of my life that matter most to me. I struggle with my marriage because it matters to me. If it didn't, I would be indifferent to those things that slowly destroy it. I struggle with my children because they matter to me. If I didn't, I would be indifferent to the choices they make even if they were detrimental to their wellbeing. I struggle with my job because it matters to me. If I didn't, I would do the absolute minimum required, punch the clock and go home. And I struggle with my faith in God because it matters to me. If I didn't, I would be indifferent, and wouldn't feel anger, regret, or guilt, nor would I feel awe, humility, wonder, intimacy, reassurance and love. Struggling indicates that something matters to us and this is the essence of life and vitality, namely that we care *enough* about something to struggle with and for it!

As the story of God's chosen people unfolds, Israel is clearly a name of destiny. Throughout her tumultuous history, Israel will struggle with its faith in God, individually and collectively. And on some level, we are heirs of the faith of Israel and therefore, heirs of the destiny inherent in the name. We too, share a destiny in which our relationship to God, if it truly matters, results in consistent struggle. There is little doubt however, that this is contrary to the trend of a culture that encourages and strives for ease in all aspects of life's complexities. Against that cultural trend is a God who names his faithful Struggles, because God knows the opposite will be for his people to embrace the slow, imperceptive, spiritual death of indifference.

The scriptures declare that struggle is good, so good in fact that God even names his chosen people, *Struggles with God* because struggling is an expression of desire and a manifestation of pining after the heart of God.

In a sense, when God says that he now calls us Israel, he is saying that he now names us "the ones who care enough about me, who care enough about our relationship, to struggle with me and actively resist indifference towards me."

So, an appropriate blessing would be:

May we always struggle with those aspects of our lives that matter most and become increasingly aware that indifference is an alarming spiritual condition that we must resist.

CHAPTER 3

Hardened Hearts & the Egyptian Death Cult

(Exodus 7)

A highlight of my life came along when I served as the Executive Director of a small one-year college in the beautiful country of Ecuador. As an international school, we would often host visitors to the campus ranging from prospective students to donors to government dignitaries. In many ways the culture of Ecuador willingly adopted me and my family, so one of the many joys of my role was to observe how guests delighted in their experience. Every visitor was eager to interact with our Ecuadorian team members, relying on long-forgotten lessons from high school Spanish class or a phrase that had been learned and practiced specifically for their visit. Our Ecuadorian team, in reflection of the graciousness of the culture, indulged them and our bilingual team members patiently provided answers when incessantly asked, "How do you say—(nearly any word you might imagine)—in Spanish?"

Every good team has a prankster, and ours was Baxter, one of the faculty. He loved to teach our guests phrases that they could share with our Ecuadorian team members, like "My mother is the Queen of England," or "I look good in goat hair" or "Do you think I should shave my knees?" It would be safe to say that our multi-national team eagerly anticipated each time an unsuspecting guest came to visit.

On one such occasion, the president of the consortium of colleges to which we belonged came to visit and, as part of the festivities we made special arrangements for him to meet the mayor of the small town in which the campus was located. Baxter is nothing if not consistent and took it upon himself to coach the President on how to properly greet the Mayor, teaching him the phrase "Soy mujer" and telling him that it meant "It's an honor." Baxter explained further to the President, that "the phrase should be said with vigor, with firm conviction because," he explained, "the Ecuadorian culture responds more favorably to confidence than timidity." Wanting to make a good impression, the President practiced the phrase multiple times and when the Mayor of the town arrived on campus, Baxter introduced the two men. With the burden of international relations on his shoulders, the President strode up to the Mayor, firmly grasped his hand and with unreserved confidence stated "Soy mujer (I am a woman)!"

The Mayor's smile–and his body—froze. The visiting President, sensing something wasn't right, but assuming he had said the phrase incorrectly, tried to salvage the moment by giving it another try, only this time annunciating each syllable: "Soy mu-jer (I. Am. A. Woman!)" With the awkward moment suspended in midair, the Mayor gently withdrew his hand, took a step back and glanced toward Baxter for an explanation who, without missing a beat, met the Mayor's gaze with a shrug as if to say, "Who knew?" Baxter then turned to the President, and shaking his head slightly in feigned shock whispered, "How could you say that to the Mayor?"

The moment is indelibly etched in my mind.

The Mayor smiling and waiting for an explanation. The President glancing anxiously between the Mayor and Baxter, utterly lost and confused, and feeling somewhat betrayed because he had done what Baxter had asked and was now being thrown under the proverbial bus for it!

Though the story of Moses and Pharaoh is by far one of my favorites, I have never been completely at peace with it. It begins with Moses hiking in the wilderness and stumbling upon the prototype for non-extinguishable birthday candles, a bush that was on fire, but not burning up. As it turns out, God is within the non-burning burning bush and, after easily capturing Moses' full and undivided attention, directs him to go to Egypt so he can command all-powerful Pharaoh to let the enslaved Hebrew people go.

In other words, God desires Moses to go to Egypt, arguably the most powerful nation on earth at the time, and demand that the supreme leader, Pharaoh—someone who can have you killed on command—let his free-labor work force leave the country.

And it gets even better!

God adds this little plot twist: When Moses and his brother Aaron (whom God includes after Moses tries to use another loophole to get out of going) finish making the demand of Pharaoh, God will:

"...harden Pharaoh's heart, and though I multiply my signs and wonders in Egypt, he will not listen to you. Then I will lay my hand on Egypt and with mighty acts of judgment I will bring out my divisions, my people the Israelites." (NIV)

God commands Pharaoh to do something, then punishes him for it. How can anyone be all right with a God who, at best is being capricious, and at worst, unjust or even sadistic.

I have, however, found some peace with the story thanks to an insight provided by Randall Price in his book *The Stones Cry Out: What Archaeology Reveals About the Truth of the Bible*[4]. While not the book's main point, his thoughts provide a good background when reading the story of Pharaoh and his hard heart (Exodus 6-7). Before we delve further, we need to become aware of a biblical principle that is consistently at work throughout scripture and garner a rudimentary understanding of the thought, practice and belief surrounding death in ancient Egypt.

First, a shout-out goes to Walt Disney for the movie *Prince of Egypt*. Without that movie, a whole generation would have emerged unaware of the story of Moses because, until then, this was a generation that did not know Charlton Heston! Thankfully, now almost everyone knows the broad strokes of the Exodus story, including that God visited various plagues on the empire of Egypt in preparation for his dramatic parting of the Red Sea.

Egypt was a polytheistic culture, worshiping many gods whom they believed controlled and influenced many critical

---

4. *The Stones Cry Out* by Randall Price, Harvest House Publishers, Eugene, Oregon, 1997. Note chapter seven, focusing on the rites and practices of the Egyptian death cult.

aspects of their existence. Following is a list of some of the deities that were worshipped and, in some cases, the form in which the Egyptians believed they revealed themselves to humans[5]:

Hapi	Spirit of the Nile River	Blood in the Nile River	7:14-25
Khnum	Guardian of the Nile River	Blood in the Nile River	7:14-25
Heqt	Took the form of a frog	Frogs	8:1-5
Uatchit	Took the form of a fly	Flies	8:20-32
Ptah	Took the form of a cow	Cattle	9:1-7
Mnevis	Took the form of a cow	Cattle	9:1-7
Hathor	Took the form of a cow	Cattle	9:1-7
Sekhmet	Goddess of healing	Boils & sores on all things	9:8-11
Serapis	Goddess of healing	Boils & sores on all things	9:8-11
Seth	Protector of crops	Crops destroyed by hail	9:12-35
Nut	Sky goddess	Crops destroyed by hail	9:12-35
		Crops destroyed by locust	10:1-20
Re	Sun god	Darkness	10:21-29
Atum	God of the setting sun	Darkness	10:21-29
Osiris	Giver of life	Death of all first born	11:1-10
Pharaoh	Considered to be god	Death of all first born	11:1-10

Thinking back to God's statement to Moses about mighty acts of judgement and seeing the roster of Egyptian gods, one can almost sense the gathering storm clouds. These were the gods of the Egyptians, headed by Pharaoh, who was himself considered a god. Against this backdrop, God uses the plagues themselves to bear tragic witness to the fact that there is only one true God who alone carries all authority.

---

5. *The Stones Cry Out* by Randall Price, Harvest House Publishers, Eugene, Oregon, 1997, pg. 123.

One can almost hear God taunting the Egyptians.

"You want to worship the gods of the Nile River? Look, I turned the water into blood. Where are your Nile gods now?"

"You want to worship frogs? Let me help. Here are frogs, millions and millions of frogs."

"What's that? Flies? Let me make it easy for you to worship them. Here are millions and millions of flies."

"Oh, your gods come in the form of cattle. Did you happen to notice that those gods are now dying in droves?"

"Who is it that controls the sun itself, when it rises and sets? Is it your gods? If so, then why is there darkness during the day?"

And the tragic climax of this battle Royale…

"You believe that Pharaoh can grant and protect your life? Listen to the wailing as the first born of every family die. Where is your giver and protector of life now?"

Out of this tragic showdown between the gods of Egypt and the one true God, we see a dynamic that will recur consistently throughout the Bible, dynamics I call Biblical Principles. These principles are consistently evident throughout all of scripture and, once we are aware of them, we see them at work in the day-to-day engagement of faith. They are always at play and we live either in tension with, or often in reaction to them.

For the purpose of this passage, the biblical principle at work is that God allows us to pursue our gods, that which we at our core truly worship, even to their potentially destructive end. Whether in the book of Joshua when the Israelites cross over into the promised land, or in the book of Judges when God removes his hand, or with Elijah and the prophets of Baal, all the way to the New Testament's descriptions of the choices we make in regard to sin, God allows the double edge of free will. He allows us to pursue our false gods, that which we at our core truly worship, even to their potentially destructive end.

Take a moment to reflect on personal relationships, the organizations or businesses in which we work and even our most tragic cultural trends. Do you see this biblical principle?

No matter what the rhetoric may be to the contrary, that which is truly desired, is being pursued, sometimes to the destruction of a person, a marriage, a family, an organization, a business and yes, even a country.

This biblical principle becomes even more undeniable when placed next to what is arguably the most extravagant and tragic object lesson of all time. Once God delivers the Hebrew people from Egypt, he gathers them at the foot of Mt. Sinai where, through Moses, he gives what will become a consistent message to them:

> *"'I am the Lord your God, who brought you out of Egypt, out of the land of slavery. You shall have no other gods before me. You shall not make for yourself an image in the form of anything in heaven above or on the earth beneath or in the waters below. You shall not bow down to them or worship them; for I, the Lord your God, am a jealous God...'" (Exodus 20:1-5a, NIV)*

Against the plagues and the parting of the Red Sea, it would be safe to say that God's message is clear: Egypt had other gods that they worshiped before the one, true God, and it would be advisable for the now-free Hebrew nation to not worship other gods.

How does this apply to the hardening of Pharaoh's heart? The Bible assumes that the reader knows certain cultural and contextual realities of which the enslaved Hebrew people would have certainly been aware. Most importantly, the Hebrew people knew that the Egyptians believed Pharaoh was a god on par with (if not the ultimate manifestation of) the sun god Ra and Osiris, the givers of life. Pharaoh himself was considered the primary god of the Egyptians. Even his words were perceived as a creative force.

Additionally, the Egyptians believed that as god, Pharaoh's power was absolute, controlling not only natural elements, but history as well. Interestingly, in the first chapters of Genesis, it is God who speaks into a formless void and order comes from chaos. It is God's words that speak life into existence, making God the author of history. So, the stage for confrontation is inevitably set and God intends to write a history for the Egyptians in which this biblical principle of allowing them to pursue their gods, that which they at their core truly worship, even to their destructive end, is always at work.

But, hold that thought for a moment.

Amidst the findings unearthed through the many and various archaeological projects in Egypt is a document entitled *Book of the Dead.* In it we gain a glimpse into the thought processes and theology surrounding death and ancient burial practices of Egypt. For example, it was believed that after the body was embalmed and mummified, the deceased Pharaoh had to stand trial in the Hall of Judgment in order to determine his guilt or innocence. If judged guilty, the Pharaoh's fate was eternal destruction. If judged innocent, the fate was eternal life, with unfathomable rewards.

However, in order to assess guilt and innocence, a long list of sins would be read to the Pharaoh and he would need to declare his innocence, stating that he had not committed any of them throughout his earthly life and reign. Known as the Negative Confessions, the integrity of the test lay in the Egyptian belief that the human heart's intrinsic inclination is to tell the truth and, when pressed, the heart not only desires to confess sinfulness, but cannot help but do so. Consequently, it was believed that the heart of the Pharaoh was placed on the scales of judgment and weighed against truth.

The highlighted portion of the image below captures a rendition of this practice in Egyptian art:

According to this practice, the deceased Pharaoh would begin to give a testimony of his life in relation to the list of sins and his heart would, on the scale of judgment and truth, affirm or deny the purity of the Pharaoh's testimony. In a sense, the Pharaoh's words were verified and corroborated by the heart. If the Pharaoh spoke truth, the heart remained silent. If the Pharaoh lied, the heart could not help but speak out, thereby condemning them to eternal destruction.

For obvious reasons, the Negative Confessions was of great concern to the Pharaohs since they were under no delusion that they would be able to claim a complete and total life of purity. They also knew they could not prevent their hearts from speaking the truth. So, there emerged an ingenious way to prevent that from happening. Prior to their death, the Pharaohs would make a stone carved in the image of the sacred dung beetle and inscribe incantations on it along the lines of "do not witness against me" and "do not rebel against me." The dung beetles shape roughly mimicked that of a human heart and so, during mummification the actual heart of the Pharaoh was removed and replaced with the stone heart. The Pharaohs believed that this hard heart would remain silent during the Negative Confessions and thus not contradict the list of sins being read. Without contradiction from the heart, the scale had no alternative but to tip in favor of the Pharaoh and declare him sinless as he entered the afterlife!

Bearing that in mind, if you were Pharaoh and you believed upon death that such a judgment awaited you, what is the one thing you'd desire most, the one characteristic or trait for which you'd long, even embodying it at times throughout your mortal life? It would be a hard heart. You would want a heart that would eventually need to remain silent when the list of sins was read against you in the Negative Confessions, when eternal condemnation or rewards beyond comprehension hung in the balance. So, by hardening Pharaoh's heart, God isn't being erratic or contradictory. In fact, he is being amazingly consistent in granting Pharaoh his desire—what he truly worshiped at his core—and allowing him to pursue it ultimately to its destructive end! You can almost hear God saying, "Pharaoh, you desire at your very core to have a hard heart? I will give it to you."

The story of the hardening of Pharaoh's heart reveals one of the most misunderstood realities of the Christian faith, namely that God bestows on humanity the incredible dignity of allowing us to choose. In fact, I would suggest that the word "no" is a unique, image-of-God-bearing gift to humans and our declaration of true freedom. It is the essence of what it means to be liberated. It separates us from all other elements of the created order, making us uniquely human.

Permit me a story to illustrate what I mean.

The other day a cat wandered into our yard and my dog, upon seeing the cat, began barking and charged the unfortunate stray who equally, without thought, frantically leapt over the fence to safety. My dog saw the cat and instinctively charged. He didn't pause, take a deep centering breath, assess potential possibilities as to why the cat may have inadvertently wandered into the yard, and then, after careful deliberation, make a calm and informed decision.

He saw the cat. He charged.

Like animals, humans have instincts and impulses. Unlike animals, we can *choose* to override those instincts and impulses. I can be so angry at someone and shout "I COULD KILL YOU!" but I am not then obligated to kill the person! I don't need to yield to that impulse. Unlike an animal, I can say no to an instinct, to an impulse that would lead to unfortunate consequences.

Is it easy? No. Is it attainable? Yes. Contrary to my impulse, instinct, even overwhelming fear and a host of other possibilities and scenarios, I can choose to say "no" to acting on those impulses.

Rabbi Harold S. Kushner, one of my favorite thinkers and authors, said "...I will insist that every adult, no matter how unfortunate a childhood [they] had or how habit-ridden [they] may be, is free to make choices about [their] life. If we are not free, if we are bound by circumstances and experiences, then we are no different from the animal who is bound by instinct."[6] In other words, God bestows on humanity the incredible dignity of allowing us to choose. God also allows us to pursue our gods, that which we at our core truly worship, potentially to their destructive end.

SO, HOW DO WE AVOID DESIRING OUR OWN HARDENED heart?

By recognizing that we are not bound by instinct. We are not animals.

We are uniquely, in all creation, the bearers of God's image. So, let's act like it!

Let's shed the childish notion that "no" is oppressive, limiting and wrong, and instead embrace that it is our unique God-given ability to say "no" that makes us human!

You are not an animal, so don't act like one.

If you do, however, don't be surprised when God lets you do so to your own ultimate destruction.

---

6.   Kushnor, Harold S., "Why Bad Things Happen to Good People," pg. 83, Avon Book, New York, 1981.

CHAPTER 4

Simon & Garfunkel Had it Right

(Judges 11)

I f ever you should desire to experience the paradox of hope and despair, potty train a small child!

My wife and I recently entered a new phase of life together. With much joy and admittedly a tinge of sorrow, we officially became empty nesters. Our two daughters have begun their own lives, along with their spouses. One aspect of this phase is that we have begun to downsize, which involves sorting through the numerous boxes that hold decades of accumulated memories.

In one box we came upon a picture of one of our daughters potty training or, as is revealed in the photo, stubbornly sitting on the toilet, fists clenched and defiantly glaring at the camera.[7] The photo triggered the memory of the day we reached a critical point in this training, when her confidence to wear "big girl pants" through the night exceeded our confi-

---

7. I have opted not to identify the daughter. If you really desire to solve this mystery, I'd encourage you to get to know my children and it will then be revealed to you in short order.

dence in her ability to do so. Her persistence in wanting to try was admirable and tiring, so whether it was fair or right, we attached something that she deeply desired to the success of being able to sleep all through the night in her big girl pants. We had a family trip to the zoo planned for the weekend, and my wife and I made it exceedingly clear to our little girl that, if she didn't make it through the night without incident, not only she, but the entire family would not go to the zoo.[8]

Right or wrong (and wrong, as it turned out) we were certain that our daughter would consider her options carefully and choose wisely. Not surprisingly, she accepted the challenge.

Morning came and I, slowly and quietly opened the door to her room and…sure enough, I found her sleeping on the floor—and in the middle of her mattress was a big wet spot. She must have sensed me standing there because after a moment, she stirred, her eyes fluttered open and she sat up. She blinked a few times and then looked over at her bed, then up at me. Rather than doing a justified victory dance and more in the vein of the perfect television Dad, I walked over, knelt beside her, smiled reassuringly and asked gently, "What happened here last night?" nodding toward her bed. She bought some time by rubbing the sleep out of her eyes then, deciding that not to answer was the best answer (commonly recognized among adults as "taking the 5th"), she simply looked back at me.

Not wanting to cause her embarrassment, I gently and quietly articulated the obvious saying, "It's alright sweetie.

8. I can hear the collective groan of parents everywhere scorning our decision to tie something so wonderful as a family outing to performing a bodily function. In our defense, we were young, inexperienced parents and our daughter's stubbornness is legendary.

Maybe you're just not ready for big girl pants."

That's when it got interesting. Before I could give her a reassuring hug, she pointed to her bed and said simply, "I didn't do that."

That was unexpected! For a moment I considered engaging her in meaningful dialogue—but given the preponderance of evidence, decided to instead offer her a graceful way out. "Are you sure?" I asked with a hint of appropriate levity while injecting an equal hint of logic. "Who else could have done it?"

"Our cat" she said without hesitation, and I didn't miss the fleeting glimmer of self-satisfaction on her face, believing she had just offered an equally plausible option. And I'd be lying if I didn't say a small part of me was impressed at the deftness with which she threw our cat under the bus. So, I changed tactics and utilized rudimentary geometry, the idea of ratios and proportions to guide her toward embracing the obvious.

"That is an interesting thought, Sweetie," I offered, "but our cat is kind of small and that stain on your bed is...well, pretty big, almost as big as a two-year-old might make."

BOOM! Drop mic! Let science do the talking!

Almost as if she sensed the trap, she responded incredulously and without missing a beat "It wasn't *our* cat, Dad!" (This girl *really* wanted to go to the zoo!)

Despite knowing I shouldn't let her continue down this road, I couldn't help myself. I took the bait. "Then whose cat was it?" I asked.

"The neighbors." She replied matter-of-factly.

As I contemplated my next move, I admit that for a fleeting moment I caught myself following her logic. Our neighbors *do* have a cat and it *is* bigger! Then I caught myself and reengaged in what was evolving into a serious debate with an increasingly uncertain outcome. I chose to again employ the argument of proportions, pointing out that, though our neighbor's cat was in fact larger than ours, the stain left on her bed was still too big for even a larger cat.

My sweet little daughter promptly responded "I know, Daddy! It was their lion."

As God is my witness, I saw an unmistakable smug look on her toddler face, like she had just outmaneuvered an opposing chess player and knew she was just a few moves away from me tipping my King! (Internally, I had to grudgingly concede her ability to resolve the proportion issue on the fly: a big stain obviously needs a big cat, right? Well played little girl. Well played indeed.)

I took a breath and decided perhaps this would be a good time to summarize her position.

"So, my dear," I began. "You want me to believe that last night, after we all went to bed, our neighbors purchased a lion and that at some time during the night, their new lion somehow escaped its cage, hopped the fence, found a way to climb up to your second story bedroom window and, without waking you, remove your window screen, and climb into your room. Do I have it right so far?"

My hypothesis was met with silence, so I continued. "Then, you want me to further believe that the lion tiptoed over to your bed and, without waking you, lifted you out of bed, and set you gently on the floor. Then, the lion hopped onto your bed, peed in it and climbed back out your window, remembered to put back the screen (which I do appreciate), and returned home. Is that what you're saying happened in this room last night?"

My little daughter took a moment to think, seemingly as if to review my summary for errors. Then she nodded her head emphatically and said, "Yes!" And she added in all seriousness, "You should probably go talk to them."

CHILDREN ARE FASCINATING LITTLE CREATURES, AREN'T they? People of all ages fascinate me, especially the absurd lengths to which we will go when we want something to be true or *don't* want something to be discovered. Whether a trip to the zoo, political ambition, scandal cover-up or fiscal gain: if we feel it is in our best interest, there is no limit to the intellectual contortions and rationalizations we will pursue!

I once had the privilege of hearing a Talmud teacher present on the passage of scripture found in Judges 11, the story of Jephthah, or as he referred to it, the Indictment of Silence. Before he began, we were invited to give attention to what was *not* written in the passage rather than what was, and warned that at times, silence is *not* golden.

From the opening verses, the narrative wants you to know a few things about Jephthah, namely that his father was an accomplished warrior and Jephthah was his illegitimate child by way of a prostitute. Additionally, Gilead and his wife had several other sons who wanted nothing to do with Jephthah, especially when it came to their father's estate (one more person with which to split the money). The opening verses also relate that, when they were finally able, the half-brothers drove Jephthah away, forcing him to the land of Tob where Scripture says:

> "...*a gang of scoundrels gathered around him and followed him." (Judges 11:3, NLT)*

Scoundrels makes it sound like Jephthah became the leader of a biblical version of Our Gang; as though Jephthah were leading a gang comprised of Alfalfa, Spanky, Buckwheat and Porky! The reality is that Jephthah became the leader of a gang who marauded and robbed people. In fact, he was so good at it that he developed quite a reputation as a formidable fighter because he was the first man the elders of Gilead thought of to lead them in battle against the Ammonites when they threatened war against Israel (Judges 11:4-6).

As the story reveals, Jephthah is understandably skeptical of the Elders, recalling how they had driven him from his home (Judges 11:7). Perhaps out of desperation—or maybe the thought that, though Jephthah would put up a good fight, the Ammonites would inevitably be victorious–the leaders of Israel offer to make Jephthah not only commander of the army but ruler of all the people of Gilead. This promise, however, came with one minor caveat: Jephthah had to defeat the Ammonites.

Interestingly, Jephthah doesn't appear phased by the idea of fighting the Ammonites, but is openly skeptical of the elders and their promise. Apparently sensing his hesitation, the elders of Gilead underscore their sincerity by making a vow before God stating that, should the Ammonites be defeated, they would indeed make Jephthah ruler of all Gilead (Judges 11:10). So, on the strength and binding nature of this vow (Deuteronomy 23:23), Jephthah agrees, and assumes his role as commander of the army knowing that, should he win, he would ultimately become the ruler of Gilead.

One would think that, as the new commander, Jephthah's first order of business would be to review the troops and begin formulating battle plans. In fairness, he may, in fact have done that, but the passage does state that Jephthah sends a messenger to the king of Ammon to try to negotiate a way forward (not exactly the cut-throat, mercenary, take-no-prisoners action that the elders of Gilead had hoped for). Jephthah and the king of Ammon go back and forth in their conversation, but eventually negotiations fail, a diplomatic solution is impossible, and Jephthah leads his army into Ammonite territory.

On the eve of the battle, the passage relates that Jephthah makes a vow to the Lord.

"He said, 'If you give me victory over the Ammonites, I will give to the Lord whatever comes out of my house to meet me when I return in triumph. I will sacrifice it as a burnt offering.'" (Judges 11:30-31, NLT)

Foolish, impulsive, desperate, contemptible and rash are some of the adjectives I've heard used to describe Jephthah's vow, both in commentaries and on the two rare occasions when I've heard sermons on this passage. I understand the initial reaction. Who would be so reckless as to offer to sacrifice whatever first comes out of one's house (unless reasonably sure it would be your unemployed brother-in-law who, two years ago, only needed a place to "crash for a couple weeks!")?

Perhaps this will help. Below is an artist rendering and recreation of what a typical dwelling may have looked like during this time period.

It is important to note the two levels to the home: an upper level that housed the living quarters where a family slept, and a lower level that was used for storage, cooking and housing animals at night. Take note as well that the lower portion of the home included a half wall that created a small courtyard with a single entrance which the family locked at night after gathering their animals. This was common practice so that the animals didn't fall prey to predators or human poachers. Given that the courtyard door or gate was considered the entrance to the home, it is not unreasonable to deduce that Jephthah anticipated an animal pushing its way to the front and through the gate when it was opened and it was to be *that* animal that Jephthah was prepared to sacrifice to God, no matter how valuable. Within the context of the day, Jephthah's vow isn't foolish, short-sighted, rash or ignorant. It was a vow made in reflection of what was typical when opening a gate behind which excited, confined animals waited. Jephthah believed he was vowing to sacrifice an animal that would push and rush through the moment an opportunity afforded itself.

To continue the story, Jephthah leads his army against the Ammonites and the Lord gives him victory, crushing the Ammonites and devastating about twenty towns. In other words, Jephthah doesn't just unexpectedly win, he shockingly annihilates his enemy. Savoring the victory, he is excited to return home to be with his family, where he hopes to continue the celebration with a sacrifice of thanksgiving to the Lord. Unfortunately, as he nears his home, that hope is crushed because the first living thing that comes out through the courtyard gate is not one of his animals!

> *"When Jephthah returned home to Mitzpah, his daughter came out to meet him, playing on a tambourine and dancing for joy. She was his one and only child; he had no other sons or daughters." (Judges 11:34, NLT)*

You can almost hear the despair in Jephthah's words.

> *"When [Jephthah] saw her, he tore his clothes in anguish. 'Oh, my daughter!' he cried out. 'You have completely destroyed me! You've brought disaster on me! For I have made a vow to the Lord, and I cannot take it back.' And she said, 'Father, if you have made a vow to the Lord, you must do to me what you've vowed, for the Lord has given you a great victory over your enemies, the Ammonites.'" (Judges 11:35-36, NLT)*

I would like to suggest to you that a *LOT* probably happened between verses 35 and 36 that the Bible didn't record. The way it reads, it's almost as if Jephthah's daughter is nonchalant about the whole matter which, most assuredly she would not be. At the very least I am certain that Jephthah's wife had a few choice thoughts to share with him, probably along the lines of "You WHAT?!" followed by bargaining, pleading, wailing, weeping, cursing, and Jephthah spending more than a few nights sleeping down below with the animals. Regardless, the statement of needing to remain faithful to a vow made to the Lord remains.

In whatever manner Jephthah, his daughter and family finally accept the reality of needing to keep the vow, and Jephthah's daughter makes only one request before her father follows through on his vow to the Lord, namely that she be permitted to…

> "…go up and roam in the hills and weep with my friends for two months, because I will die a virgin." (Judges 11:37, NLT)

Jephthah grants her permission, and Scripture goes on to say that she and her friends went into the hills and wept because she would not live to be a mother, she would never have her own children or experience the blessing of raising a family. In short, she and her friends were mourning that she would not get to live out her life. For two months, she and her friends wandered around Gilead weeping in anticipation of her being sacrificed.

This group of women wandered and wept—for two months.

Two entire months!

For sixty days this group was wandering, mourning and wailing in anticipation of the coming sacrifice of Jephthah's daughter.

It's almost as if Scripture wants to emphasize just how long this group of young women wandered around Gilead and, I suggest that is exactly what the Bible wants the reader to note.

Think about it for a moment. The Bible assumes that you know that Gilead was a geographic area that was at most, 40 miles long and 20 miles wide, dotted with towns whose population did not exceed 150-200 residents. For *two months* Jephthah's daughter and her friends wandered this small area weeping and crying because Jephthah was going to fulfill his to vow to the Lord and sacrifice his daughter.

By way of personal experience and for comparison, I lived for seven years in a small Canadian prairie town of 4,000 and I assure you that it was impossible to sneeze on the east side of the town without someone from the west side sending you a bowl of chicken soup within fifteen minutes!

If a group of women walked around that small Canadian town for two months weeping and lamenting the fact that the father of one of them was going to kill her, I assure you that every single person in the town and surrounding 40-mile radius would have known about it, even without the modern conveniences of cell phones, social media, texting and email! This is the Bible's way of saying that *every* single person in Gilead knew what was about to happen *before* it happened.

Yet, after two months passed, scripture says...

"When she returned home, her father kept the vow he had made, and she died a virgin." (Judges 11:39, NLT)

Let's be clear on this point, so there is no wiggle room.

He did it.

Jephthah sacrificed his daughter and everyone in the greater Gilead metro area not only knew it was going to happen, but without a doubt knew when it was over, too.

So, ON THAT CHEERY NOTE, LET'S RETURN TO THE ORIGI-
nal question of the Talmudic teacher: what is not being
stated in this story? What is glaringly conspicuous by virtue
of its absence?

The answer is both simple and revealing.

What is missing are the elders of Gilead, who were so
prominent at the beginning of the story. The leaders who
approached Jephthah in the beginning are suddenly nowhere
to be found.

Where did they go? They had such a prominent and
pivotal role in the beginning of the story, but by the end,
they seem to have vanished.

What else is missing? You will recall, the leaders of
Gilead made a vow too, that if Jephthah won, they would
make him ruler over all Gilead. This was a key piece for
Jephthah, so it seems reasonable to assume that Jephthah's
ascension to the position of ruler would be noted. Instead,
there is a deafening silence. Only Jephthah's fulfillment of
his vow is recorded.

In the next chapter (Judges 12), the people appear to
be following Jephthah, as he addressed Ephraim and their
lack of support during the Ammonite conflict. Judges 12:7
notes that Jephthah led Israel for six years before dying.
Yet there is absolutely nothing to indicate that the elders
of Gilead—the religious leaders—fulfilled their vow to the
Lord, officially making Jephthah the ruler of all Gilead.

Why? Because the elders of Gilead did not want Jephthah
to be their leader!

In fact, they didn't even want him as a neighbor because
you'll recall, they chased him out of Gilead! It's as if the
religious leaders took a posture that if Jephthah didn't bring
up the whole "ruler-of-Gilead" thing, neither would they.

Unfortunately, something more insidious is at work within their silence, and in order to gain deeper context, I share this insight by scholar and Rabbi, Joseph Telushkin who writes that one "...of the Torah's earliest teachings is that God abhors human sacrifice (Genesis 22), a point it repeatedly makes (Leviticus 18:21, 20:1-5; Deuteronomy 12:31, 18:10)."[9]

Given the deep rootedness of this biblical truth, and despite how morally depraved Israel may have sunk at this point in the narrative, such a vow violates this biblical law banning human sacrifice. Consequently, this vow should never have been made or, more to the point, should never have been *allowed* to be made, let alone carried out! To further this point, the Talmud teacher to whom I referred in the beginning stated that God would never have even heard; in other words, would never have validated or received such a vow because it was so contrary to God's nature. Yet, we are left with the horrific truth that, not only did Jephthah sacrifice his daughter to honor a vow he made to the Lord, but everyone in Gilead knew he was going to do it—and did nothing to prevent it!

Why?

Why would the people of Gilead—or more to the point—the elders of Gilead who absolutely knew better, allow Jephthah to do something so abhorrent in the eyes of God?

Unfortunately, one must think deviously to find the answer, (and if you are like my wife, purer in motive and heart than me, the answer isn't obvious because such people are simply incapable of thinking treacherously).

---

9.   Pg. 177, *Biblical Literacy: The Most Important People, Events, and Ideas of the Hebrew Bible* by Rabbi Joseph Telushkin, William Morrow, An Imprint of Harper Collins Publishers, 1997.

According to this Talmud teacher, the elders of Gilead remained quiet because they did not want—nor did they *ever* want—Jephthah to rule. Therefore, to their twisted way of thinking, by letting Jephthah sacrifice his daughter and staying silent as he sacrificed a human who bears the image of God, they believed he would have so violated God's command and biblical law, that he would be rendered unfit and ineligible to rule Israel. In other words, the elders of Gilead, those religious leaders of the entire town, remained silent while something abhorrent to God was carried out because it supported their selfish personal and political desires.

That is what is *not* written and what stands out through the deafening sound of the silence.

Where were the voices to speak out and stop this sacrifice, a sacrifice that God clearly finds abhorrent and is clearly in violation of the biblical law?

How did these leaders look at themselves in the proverbial mirror and remain silent? We know they couldn't claim that they didn't know what was going to happen, because Jephthah's daughter and friends wandered and proclaimed their intent for two solid months!

This leads us to another biblical principle that is at work throughout the whole of Scripture. This principle will not be without its critics, because it has a collective nature to it that is contrary to the wildly individualistic perspective of our American culture, but its biblical truth is persistent.

The biblical principle is this: to remain silent in the presence of sin is to sin. Silence in the face of sin means we are as culpable as the those directly involved.

LET THAT SINK IN FOR A MOMENT.

Let that sink in as we recall the times that we have turned away from a situation that we knew was wrong, reassuring ourselves in the quiet of our core that it was "none of our business."

Let that sink in as we think about the values that we as a culture collectively hold, and what they look like when measured against the life and example of Jesus Christ. Then observe the futility of seeking hallow reassurance in the mantra of "at-least-I'm-not-as-bad-as."

Let that sink in as we remain silent when people of the faith find their identity in race, ethnicity, nation, socioeconomic class or gender before they find it in the one who deems *all* humans as unique bearers of the image of God.

Let that sink in when those same people of faith remain silent when a vocal segment of professed brothers and sisters are permitted to spiritualize the demonization of a specific people, the exultation of one ethnic group as more powerful or superior to another, remaining silent when an alleged proponent of the faith regularly demeans, pathologically lies, degrades, gaslights, bullies, and questions the faith of others; remaining silent at the dehumanization of people by referencing them as an invasion, or outright replacing their God-given humanity for the term evil.

Let that sink in as we falsely believe that if we, as individuals are righteous, we will somehow be spared the horrors we are certain will be rained down on those we deem unrighteous. Instead, think about how many Old Testament prophets suffered the consequences of God's collective judgement even though those prophets themselves were individually righteous. Their righteousness did *not* spare them the consequences of collective judgement. Nor will ours.

To remain silent in the presence of sin is to sin.

Whether or not he realized it, Paul Simon captured the truth of this biblical principle in the lyrics of his well-known song entitled *Sound of Silence*:

"Fools," said I, "You do not know
Silence, like a cancer grows."

CHAPTER 5

Getting Stoned & Grabbing the Tassel

(Luke 8)

Our youngest daughter was born as video cameras were becoming more affordable, portable and common. So, of course I had a video camera strategically (and tastefully) placed on a tripod, recording my wife as she gave birth to our second daughter. As with our first, this too was a difficult birth in which we almost lost our daughter Thanks to video, however, the gut-wrenching experience is now preserved for posterity—though to be honest, we don't watch it that often because it's not the icebreaker I thought it would be.

The camera was placed behind my wife, so the viewer can see the back of her head, me sitting to her right, the privacy curtain and then of course, the doctor and attending nurse. Even my wife agrees that it was sensitively and strategically placed, despite disagreeing that we had agreed to record the delivery. When you play back the video, in the bottom right hand corner, you can see a digital clock with hours, minutes and seconds ticking by, providing a running time stamp of events, including the exact time that Sheryl made one last herculean push with a simultaneous scream that would frighten the bravest Navy SEAL! Next, you can see our daughter being held by the doctor who passes her off screen to other medical personnel. You also see my unheralded and unmatched heroics as I unselfishly encourage my wife to breath, now that she passed the equivalent of a bowling ball (not all heroes wear capes…or give birth for that matter!).

It's my wife who first notices the quiet. She takes a deep breath, opens her eyes and asks no one in particular, "Why isn't she crying?" The seconds tick by on the time stamp in the bottom right hand corner as the nurse comes into view next to me and reassures her that everything is all right.

But the seconds tick by.

"She should be crying, shouldn't she?" my wife asks the nurse as the doctor looks off screen to the medical professional to whom he had just handed our daughter. The nurse reassures my wife again, but now her gaze too is off screen.

And the seconds tick by.

My wife's anxiety mounts as she attempts to push herself up in the bed to get a better look. Her voice captures her urgency, wanting to know about our daughter and again asks, "Why isn't she crying?" I'm holding my wife's hand tightly as she shoots a quick, worried glance toward me, but I am now standing looking offscreen, trying to see what is happening so I can answer her.

And the seconds tick by.

"She should be crying!" my wife exclaims as the doctor stands and quickly moves off screen to assist. "Why isn't she crying? She needs to cry!" my wife implores, and now everyone still in frame is looking offscreen.

And the seconds continue to tick by.

Then, you hear a loud breath, followed by a robust burst of crying that to this day, remains one of the sweetest sounds these two parents will ever hear.

Even as I recount this to you, my heart rate quickens, my blood pressure rises, and my breathing becomes constrained. I've never felt more helpless or more powerless than I did during those long minutes, forever ensconced on a video tape with a time stamp in the corner that seems to mock me whenever I watch it.

I remember fighting back the panic!

I remember the horrible thoughts of what might be transpiring offscreen and thinking, "No!" shouting in silence to God to not allow my daughter to die.

I recall bargaining with God and thinking "What is it she needs? Take it from me! Whatever it is, take it from my body, even if it means my own death." It was the first time I encountered the truth that one is never more alive than when one is willing to die for something. With the possibility of death, my life suddenly became more alive.

In my faith journey, I've come to accept that opposites are always, to some degree, present. In fact, opposites must exist because they not only define one another, they also give insight and meaning to one another. Most importantly, opposites tether us to the center, preventing us from oversimplifying the complexities of what it means to be human. Can one truly understand the essence of joy without sorrow, hope without despair, peace without conflict, love without hate, light without darkness, forgiveness without judgement, and life without death? The list could go on in perpetuity but suffice it to say that the opposite in human existence is always to some degree present so that we can access and understand the richness and depth of the human experience.

As has been shared numerous times, one of the difficulties in reading the Bible is that it assumes the reader understands certain cultural and religious ideas, nuances and symbols that were prevalent when the words were written more than two thousand years ago. While it is still possible to glean truth and insight without knowing these nuances, absent them, the depth and richness of scripture is incomplete.

As we prepare to look at a story from the Gospel of Luke, I want to share this image of a man wearing a prayer shawl:

God commanded the people of Israel to wear tassels on the four corners of their garments.

"'Give the following instructions to the people of Israel: Throughout the generations to come, you must make

tassels for the hems of your clothing and attach them with a blue cord." (Numbers 15:38, NLT)

"You must put four tassels on the hem of the cloak with which you cover yourself—on the front, back, and sides." (Deuteronomy 22:12, NLT)

Why did God command this?

*"When you see the tassels, **you will remember and obey all the commands of the Lord** instead of following your own desires and defiling yourselves, as you are prone to do." (Numbers 15:39, NLT, emphasis added)*

God commanded the Israelites to wear these tassels so that they would remember to obey all the commands that had been given. It was and is meant to be a mnemonic device, a visual reminder like the five knots on the tassels that can be seen in this picture:

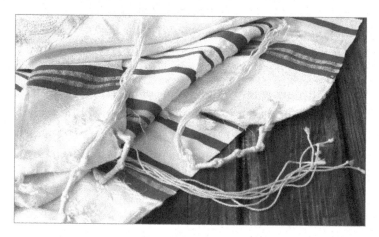

These knots represent the first five books of the Bible and what, in Judaism is called the Torah, namely the law of God as revealed to Moses and recorded in the first five books of the Hebrew scriptures (Christianity's Old Testament).

A blue thread runs through the tassel or, in some instances, is woven into the design of the prayer shawl. Blue represents the idea of holiness, being set apart, and comes to represent Israel as God's chosen nation, set apart for a specific purpose.

> *"'And you will be my kingdom of priests, my holy nation.' This is the message you must give to the people of Israel." (Exodus 19:6, NLT)*

Not coincidentally, the Apostle Peter picks up this theme in his first letter, building upon it when considering the reality of Jesus Christ.

> *"But you are not like that, for you are a chosen people. You are royal priests, a holy nation, God's very own possession. As a result, you can show others the goodness of God, for he called you out of the darkness into his wonderful light." (1 Peter 2:9, NLT)*

Apparently during Jesus' time, some of the religious leaders had made their tassels quite long in a not-so-subtle way of indicating the depth of their piety. The longer the tassel, the more pious and righteous the wearer intimated he was. Jesus referred to this in Matthew 23:5.

> *"Everything they do is for show. On their arms they wear extra wide prayer boxes with Scripture verses inside, and they wear robes **with extra-long tassels.**" (Matthew 23:5, NLT, emphasis added)*

As happens over time in most languages and cultures, the formal or literal meaning of a word or phrase comes to mean something else. For example, when my great uncle, who lived to be 91, was happy, he'd tell people he was feeling gay! It wasn't his fault that the culture had shifted around him and the word took on a very different meaning from when he was a child. During Jesus' time, these tassels were referred to as the wings of the garment, and eventually a connection emerged between these wings on the garment of pious, righteous men and the idea that those wings would contain the healing power of the Messiah. This was probably in reflection of certain passages of scripture like Malachi 4:2.

> "But you who fear my name, the Sun or Righteousness will rise with **healing in his wings**. And you will go free, leaping with joy like calves let out to pasture." (Malachi 4:2, NLT, emphasis added)

Let's add one more idea that the scriptures assume the reader of today already knows. Woven into the collective Jewish theological psyche was the belief that the coming Messiah and the one who would save and restore the nation of Israel, would in some way come from within the nation of Israel. They held that God would raise up a conquering Messiah from within the Jewish population in the spirit of David and Elijah.

When you consider this context, you can see why Jesus had something to say to those men touting their piety and righteousness by wearing long tassels because, in effect, they were walking about and, by virtue of their long tassels, their wings, were intimating something along the lines of, "Maybe it's me. Check out my long wings. I'm pretty pious, so perhaps God will choose me to be the Messiah." The words of Jesus in Matthew 23:5 make even more sense against this backdrop.

Bearing all this in mind, let's look at a couple passages of Scripture that now take on new meaning.

> *"Just then a woman who had suffered for twelve years with constant bleeding came up behind him. She touched the fringe of his robe, for she thought 'If I can just touch his robe, I will be healed.' Jesus turned around, and when he saw her, said 'Daughter, be encouraged! Your faith has made you well." And the woman was healed at that moment." (Matthew 9:20-22, NLT)*

It is fair to deduce that this passage is referring to the fringe of his robe, the tassels or the *wings* of his garment.

Luke, in his gospel, elaborates on this incident with the woman.

> *"As Jesus went with him, he was surrounded by crowds. A woman in the crowd had suffered for twelve years with constant bleeding, and she could find no cure. Coming up behind Jesus, she touched the fringe of his robe. Immediately, the bleeding stopped.*
>
> *'Who touched me?" Jesus asked.*
>
> *Everyone denied it, and Peter said, 'Master, this whole crowd is pressing up against you.'*
>
> *But Jesus said, 'Someone deliberately touched me, for I felt healing power go out from me.' When the*

> *woman realized that she could not stay hidden, she*
> *began to tremble and fell to her knees in front of*
> *him. The whole crowd heard her explain why she*
> *had touched him and that she had been immediately*
> *healed. 'Daughter,' he said to her, 'your faith has made*
> *you well. Go in peace.'" (Luke 8:42b-48, NLT)*

The tension of this passage lies in the fact that it was beyond improper for this woman to be near anyone because, according to religious law, she was considered unclean.[10] Not only that, but anything she touched would also be considered unclean, and so to avoid contaminating others, she was to be cut off from the community. Furthermore, it was *her* responsibility to not contaminate others and, having been hemorrhaging for twelve years it is highly likely that she was existing in a state of financial ruin. Due to the isolation, one might imagine that the woman was shamefully conditioned to see herself as dirty, soiled and less than human, and her community had undoubtedly reinforced that image.

Yet, here she is, clearly within a crowd of people, no doubt rubbing against others, effectively rendering them unclean. Regardless, she deliberately reaches out to touch Jesus or, at least touch the hem, the tassels of his garment.

While there is debate about the punishment for violating the laws governing cleanliness ranging from being ostracized to flogging, there is little doubt that the woman felt very afraid when Jesus stopped and asked who touched him:

---

10.   The laws that governed uncleanness for women can be found in Chapters 12 and 15 of the book of Leviticus.

> "When the woman realized that she could not stay hidden, she began to tremble and fell to her knees in front of him. The whole crowd heard her explain why she had touched him and that she had been immediately healed." (Luke 8:47, NLT)

By reaching out and grabbing the tassels on Jesus' garment, what was this woman really saying and doing?

These passages will help:

> "Everything they do is for show...they wear robes with extra-long tassels." (Matthew 23:5, NLT)

And

> "But you who fear my name, the Sun of Righteousness will rise with healing in his wings. And you will go free, leaping with joy like calves let out to pasture." (Malachi 4:2, NLT)

The woman's grasping at the tassels, or the wings of Jesus' garment was not suggesting that she believed that Jesus' clothes had some sort of magical healing powers. It was a declaration that she believed Jesus was the Messiah. In other words, in answer to the implied question behind the long tassels or wings, "Is it him? Might this be the Messiah?" The woman says, "Yes!" Pushing through a crowd against all cultural norms, risking punishment, is a desperately brave declaration of "Yes! I believe you are the Messiah!" Furthermore, her desperate declaration is confirmed as her twelve-year nightmare comes to an end because she is healed!

Remember: it was thought that the Messiah's wings would bring healing, and, at that moment, they did–confirming her belief and declaration of faith.

When she touched Jesus' wings, those tassels on his garment, Jesus felt healing power go out of him, He turned and asked who deliberately touched him. With everyone pressing in to be close to Jesus, it seems that now everyone steps back and begins to deny it. In fact, Peter implies that Jesus' question of who touched him is a bit unrealistic given the size of the crowd in which they were immersed.

Somehow, however, her identity is revealed—and when it is, the crowd quickly steps away from her, without doubt a bit stunned to learn that an unclean woman has been in their midst. Then, all eyes turn to Jesus to see what he would do next.

In my mind's eye, I see a terrified woman looking up at Jesus who, with just a simple, reassuring look into her eyes, confirms that her desperate declaration is correct. He *is* the Messiah and instant healing is proof. Instead of spelling it out for the crowd, I imagine Jesus smiling down at her as she knowingly smiles back, both instantly privy to a silent, shared understanding soon to be revealed to the observers. Then Jesus, ever-so-slightly nods his head before declaring "Your faith has made you well."

Notably, the Bible doesn't record anything happening to the woman by way of punishment.

Why?

Because she wasn't!

Instead, something infinitely more important occurred. I believe everyone who witnessed this interaction between the woman and Jesus suddenly put it all together.

The woman was suffering and needed healing.

She touched Jesus' wings and was healed.

The Messiah would have healing in his wings and, Jesus, although most likely *not* wearing ostentatiously long wings, provides an answer to the implied question. "Is it me? Could I be the Messiah?" Without a word, the interaction between Jesus and the woman screams "Yes! I am the Messiah!"

So why does the scripture not record any punishment of the unclean woman who was breaking the law by being near clean people and touching a Rabbi? Because the punishment didn't happen.

Maybe they forgot to punish her because they were too stunned by Jesus' non-verbal declaration of being the Messiah! How does one scream for justice toward an unclean, cast-aside woman when the long-awaited Messiah just revealed himself!

How I wish scripture had told us this woman's name, this woman of rugged desperation. Hope and despair existing in poignant tension, life and death in the balance, and restoration or isolation defining her future in one anguished, brief encounter. I want to know her name and the rest of her story!

Then there is Jesus, extending and embodying respect to a disgraced, ostracized woman, shrugging off right-thinking and propriety to, not only preserve her dignity, but in a fleeting moment, restore her—not just to her community, but to humanity.

There stands Jesus, who with just six words, a knowing smile and joyful glimmer in his eye declares to all observing the encounter that he is the Messiah and more importantly, declares to this woman that she is *not* dirty, soiled, defiled or filthy. She is *not* cast out or aside. She is *not* repulsive or less-than-human.

She is, in fact restored!
She is clean and whole!

WHAT KIND OF LOVE ELICITS SUCH DETERMINED, RUGGED hope?
What kind of love compels someone to shrug off conventionality and propriety?
What kind of love encourages someone to risk punishment by defying ungodly and immoral laws?
What kind of love calls to the disenfranchised, the outcast, the humiliated, the despairing in such a way as to say, "Come to me!" "It is safe!" "Take my hand!" "I will accept you!" "I am not repulsed by you *or* your behavior!"
Simply put, that kind of love is the love of Christ.
This is the sort of love that compelled Jesus to sacrifice his life for others, and the same sacrificial love and action to which those who ache and long for intimacy with God are invited. It is a love and intimacy with God that, once experienced, compels individuals to hunger, ache and long for more.
This is a love and intimacy with God that compels those who claim to be disciples of Jesus to understand that their actions, individually and collectively bring the Kingdom of Heaven near to earth, here and now, not later!
This is a love and intimacy with God that inspires those who claim to be disciples of Jesus to cultivate holy habits because the best criticism of the bad is the living of the better.
This is a love and intimacy with God that demands that those who claim to be disciples of Jesus reject *anything* that demeans, deprives or disregards human need and suffering, *especially* if there are laws or systems that exacerbate that need or perpetuate that suffering.

This is a love and intimacy with God that demands that those who claim to be disciples of Jesus understand it is not enough to have a personal relationship with Jesus if one's actions or rhetoric, whether overt or through silence and complicity, encourage, allow, or defend degradation, marginalization, misogyny, division or hate of any group of people.

This is a love and intimacy with God that demands of those who claim to be of Jesus, to lose sight of all else, focusing only on the wings of his garment and our need to grab them daily, declaring once again "It is you, Jesus. Only you!"

CHAPTER 6

Martha Stewart Ain't No Bedouin

(Luke 11)

One of my favorite comedy movies of all time is *My Big, Fat, Greek Wedding.*

I grew up in a pretty tight, all Czechoslovakian neighborhood where (1) my sister married the boy down the block (Czech married Czech, and the extended family cheered); (2) my brother married the girl across the street (Czech married Czech, and the extended family cheered); and (3) I married a girl who was Swedish and Norwegian with a hint of German, and the extended family grew pensive, wondering what tragedy of biblical proportions was about to transpire. My wife and I have now been married for over thirty years, and it would be safe to say that my extended family has finally deemed her acceptable (and those that didn't have died, so it was simply a matter of outlasting them). How do I know this? Because my grandmother grudgingly declared on our tenth wedding anniversary, "For not being Czech, she's not too bad."

One especially meaningful and funny scene from the movie is when all the female relatives of Toula, the main character who has fallen in love with a non-Greek man, stop by Toula's house because they heard her boyfriend was there.

When Toula answers the door, all her aunts, grandmothers, and nieces are on the front step, straining to see around Toula and catch a glimpse of the boyfriend. Smiling, one aunt leans forward and asks, "Is he here?" Toula shyly smiles and nods toward Ian, standing a few feet away. Then, in unison, this gaggle of excited Greek women turn and shout "Ian!" as they flood past Toula and form a ring around Ian asking questions and making comments to one another. The scene leaves little doubt that they have completely accepted him into the family. If Toula likes him, then they all like him too!

In some ways, this mirrored my own experience growing up since most of my extended family lived within a few miles of each other. We were all significantly involved in one another's lives, and it took very little to summon the family together for a party or a backyard barbeque. Any friends brought to these gatherings were immediately welcomed and added into the family. I would *not* be exaggerating when I say that, if a former student or congregational member of mine showed up at my parents' home and introduced themselves, they'd more than likely be invited in, showered with Czech hospitality that would include mountainous plates of food, a myriad of drinks, copious amounts of laughter, incredibly intrusive questions and active lobbying for support in any of the ongoing family arguments! They would be made to feel a part of our family—that is, unless they criticized a relative — because, while we all know that our uncle is crazy, he's *our* crazy uncle, so don't cross that line!

THERE WAS A SEASON OF MY LIFE WHEN I LED EDUCATIONAL pilgrimages to the land of the Bible, the current State of Israel, territory of Palestine and country of Jordan. As part of the experience, we would stay with a Bedouin community in the desert for a night or two to learn about their history, lifestyle and customs. Many of their customs and traditions are evident in the Bible and, once again, the Bible assumes that readers today are familiar with these customs. It was through these instructional adventures that I was introduced to what I believe is the closest thing I will ever experience to the biblical idea of hospitality.

Bedouins were and are people of the land whose livelihood typically entailed raising and herding livestock. Due to the scarcity of water and permanent pastoral land for grazing, they were constantly on the move. For that reason, they tended to be isolated from civilization and came to be what we North Americans might call a "hardy breed." Bedouins were extremely self-reliant —and they needed to be! In order to survive the harsh demands of the desert, the whole family, when of ability and age, engaged in any number of the critical day-to-day tasks required for living and survival. The closest parallel in the history of the United States would be those families who homesteaded during the early-to-late 1800s. They too pursued a similar, harsh lifestyle of self-sufficiency and subsistence agriculture, requiring all family members who were physically able and of age to pitch in to help the family survive.

Like the homesteaders of the 1800s, the Bedouins of the Bible relied on themselves, their families and the nearest, distant neighbors to survive. In fact, anyone who lived a similar lifestyle recognized the need—or rather, the obligation—to help their neighbors whenever required, because one never knew when the harsh conditions would change, and they would find themselves in need of neighborly assistance at a critical moment.

Innate to this survival ethos, there arose within the Bedouin culture a form of hospitality that we can begin to—
but never fully—understand. In our culture, the bar of
hospitality is set by such individuals as Martha Stewart
(someone I don't think we'd deem as hardy) and the idea
of hospitality as the highest form of human virtue is almost
unfathomable Extending hospitality to someone, especially
a stranger, became an indicator of one's integrity, depth
of character and maturity of faith. In short, a hospitable
person earned and warranted deep respect and obedience
to such an extent that extending hospitality to the stranger
came to be understood as a way to potentially encounter
divinity. This idea is behind such scripture references as
Hebrews 13:2.

> *"Don't forget to show hospitality to strangers, for some
> who have done this have entertained angels without
> realizing it!" (Hebrews 13:2, NLT)*

As was explained by our various instructors and ambassadors of the Bedouin culture, whenever a stranger came upon a Bedouin encampment, they would immediately be directed to the tent of the patriarch of the family so they could present themselves and be introduced to the extended family. Since the stranger was in route between cities, they likely had news of the outside world, a world from which the Bedouin lifestyle was isolated. The patriarch would invite the stranger to have coffee and, using his grinder (see picture below), pound the beans into powder using a distinctive rhythm that identified to the surrounding families at which tent to gather.[11]

Once everyone had gathered, coffee would be served and enjoyed while the visitor updated everyone on the news and happenings of the city or cities he had visited.

---

11.   Go to YouTube.com and search under "Bedouin Coffee Grinder" to get a sense of how the rhythm sounded when simultaneously grounding coffee beans.

Once this report was finished, the Patriarch would take out a sword which symbolized both power and protection. Given the vulnerable nature of existence in the desert, the Patriarch would symbolically hand the sword of his family to the guest or the head of the visiting family thereby indicating that, for the duration of their stay, they were to be considered part of the family and under his protection. This burden of protection was so great that it was considered the ultimate shame to withhold hospitality to someone, and of even greater shame if harm came to the guest or guests while under the family's protection.

As hard as this burden of sacrificial protection is for us to fathom, this dynamic is at work in such difficult passages as Genesis 19:1-8 where Lot sacrifices his two virgin daughters to the mob, and Judges 19:12-24 where the old man offers his virgin daughter when facing similar circumstance. In fact, in Judges 19:23-24 we see the burden of protection at work when the old man steps outside to confront those from the village who are demanding he turn over his guests:

> "*The old man stepped outside to talk to them. 'No, my brothers, don't do such an evil thing. For this man is a guest in my house, and such a thing would be shameful.'*" (Judges 19:23, NLT)

Let's face it, Martha Stewart did not have this in mind when she set the bar for hospitality at silk napkins and fancy desserts. It certainly hasn't been the measure of my commitment to hospitality either.

Once the ritual of protection was complete, a feast would begin and there would be music, dancing and more food than could possibly be consumed. The guest, or the head of the visiting clan, would be treated like a king, as this photo of one of my students and me illustrates (which later became my expected norm for students on how to treat me—wanting, of course, only for them to better embrace "biblical truth"):

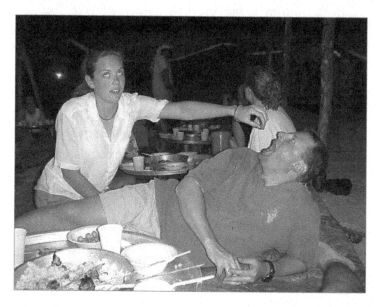

There is a very familiar passage of scripture that had always confused me but, after grasping this idea of the burden of hospitality, has since become clear.

> "Once Jesus was in a certain place praying. As he finished, one of his disciples came to him and said, "Lord, teach us to pray, just as John taught his disciples."
>
> Jesus said, "This is how you should pray:
> "Father, may your name be kept holy. May your Kingdom come soon.

Give us each day the food we need, and forgive us our sins, as we forgive those who sin against us.

And don't let us yield to temptation.

Then, teaching them more about prayer, he used this story: "Suppose you went to a friend's house at midnight, wanting to borrow three loaves of bread. You say to him, 'A friend of mine has just arrived for a visit, and I have nothing for him to eat.' And suppose he calls out from his bedroom, 'Don't bother me. The door is locked for the night, and my family and I are all in bed. I can't help you.' But I tell you this—though he won't do it for friendship's sake, if you keep knocking long enough, he will get up and give you whatever you need because of your shameless persistence.

"And so I tell you, keep on asking, and you will receive what you ask for. Keep on seeking, and you will find. Keep on knocking, and the door will be opened to you. For everyone who asks, receives. Everyone who seeks, finds. And to everyone who knocks, the door will be opened.

"You fathers—if your children ask[e] for a fish, do you give them a snake instead? Or if they ask for an egg, do you give them a scorpion? Of course not! So if you sinful people know how to give good gifts to your children, how much more will your heavenly Father give the Holy Spirit to those who ask him."
(Luke 8:1-13, NLT)

I have lost track of how many times I've heard pastors preach on this passage, and they consistently draw the application that this is about being persistent in our prayer life, about being tenacious and unwavering. In fact, in my experience Luke 11:9-10 are some of the most often quoted verses by people of the faith:

"And so, I tell you, keep on asking, and you will receive what you ask for. Keep on seeking, and you will find. Keep on knocking, and the door will be opened to you. For everyone who asks, receives. Everyone who seeks, finds. And to everyone who knocks, the door will be opened." (Luke 11:9-10, NLT)

The point of the passage does seem clear.

Don't give up!

Don't let your faith waver!

Keep on keepin' on!

There's no doubt that this interpretation of the passage rhymes with our innate North American, blue-collar work ethic and our respect for those who pull themselves up by their bootstraps, doesn't it? It tends to match that oft-quoted non-biblical phrase of "God helps those who help themselves."

This idea is reinforced through such pearls of wisdom as:

Persistence pays!

Never take "no" for an answer!

If at first, you don't succeed...

The squeaky wheel...

The tension I have with this seemingly traditional interpretation of the passage is that it means, on some level, we are to act like spoiled, impetuous children who want what we want. It's as if we are being encouraged to keep pestering God, keep petitioning him over and over and over, and then God, like a frazzled and harried parent, will eventually cave and give us what we want for no other reason than to shut us up! Does that sound like the heart of God or, more directly, is that the sort of image we have of God, a harried, on-the-verge-of-a-breakdown parent whose child badgers them into acquiescence?

While persistent prayer is a discipline or practice from which I would not dissuade anyone, it is certainly not the point of this passage.

Recall these concepts about Bedouin hospitality extended amid the harsh conditions of the desert:

- If a guest should show up—even unannounced—and need shelter and food, you are obligated to provide it

- To fail in either of these obligations was shameful, and

- One's efforts to extend hospitality spoke to the depth and maturity of one's faith.

In Luke 11:1 we see that the disciples have just asked Jesus to teach them how to pray, so Jesus teaches them what many Christian traditions refer to as "The Lord's Prayer." However, after teaching them how to pray, Jesus goes on to share two examples that give insight into the heart and posture of the one *to whom* the disciples are praying.

Let's read Jesus' first example with a different lens:

"Then, teaching them more about prayer, he used this story: "Suppose you went to a friend's house at midnight, wanting to borrow three loaves of bread. You say to him, 'A friend of mine has just arrived

for a visit, and I have nothing for him to eat.' And suppose he calls out from his bedroom, 'Don't bother me. The door is locked for the night, and my family and I are all in bed. I can't help you.' But I tell you this—though he won't do it for friendship's sake, if you keep knocking long enough, he will get up and give you whatever you need because of your shameless persistence.

"And so I tell you, keep on asking, and you will receive what you ask for. Keep on seeking, and you will find. Keep on knocking, and the door will be opened to you. For everyone who asks, receives. Everyone who seeks, finds. And to everyone who knocks, the door will be opened.(Luke 8:5-10, NLT)

The shock value of this first little parable is the fact that the friend to whom the man goes at midnight for help couldn't be bothered to get up and assist!

Knowing the obligation to extend hospitality to an unexpected guest, the friend nevertheless dismissed him saying "I can't help you," meaning he didn't *want* to be inconvenienced, going so far as to cast his reason as not wanting to disturb his family! The spotlight is *not* on the man who came at midnight to ask for help, but on the friend who refused to help!

The parable then goes on to exhort the man seeking help to keep knocking, encouraging him to make a loud scene in the middle of the quiet night by banging on the man's door until he fulfills his obligation to help. The parable says that this shameless persistence will compel the friend to get out of bed and assist him!

Some translations read that the friend will get up and help the man because his reputation is at stake! In other words, the friend will get his lazy butt out of bed and help the man because he doesn't want the community to wake up and learn that he didn't help in the first place! In a culture that deems welcoming strangers as the highest form of virtue, he didn't want to be known as the unfaithful and spiritually immature slacker who refused to help honor the unexpected guest!

You can almost hear Jesus saying to his disciples, "C'mon! When you pray, do you really think God is like the friend who won't even be bothered to get out of bed? Do you really think you need to shame God into acting in response to your prayers?"

Jesus underscores this with what I believe to be a wonderful bit of sarcasm.

> *"You fathers—if your children ask[e] for a fish, do you give them a snake instead? Or if they ask for an egg, do you give them a scorpion? Of course not! So if you sinful people know how to give good gifts to your children, how much more will your heavenly Father give the Holy Spirit to those who ask him."* *(Luke 8:11-13, NLT)*

Perhaps this is more of a reflection on my own personality, but can't you just hear the sarcasm in Jesus' words?

"Seriously, people! Do you think God is like a father that gives a snake to his son when he asks for a fish, or a scorpion when he asks for an egg? Seriously?!"

Then Jesus drives home the point that if people—who are nothing like God—know how to properly respond when a request is made of them, wouldn't it stand to reason that

God would be more than capable of responding appropriately when we pray (implied answer: yes, God would)?

This is a significantly different take-away than is typically given for this passage, and it is as true today for those who follow Jesus and pine after God as it was for the faithful Bedouins over 5,000 years ago!

DO NOT MISS THE GOSPEL MESSAGE WRAPPED INTO THIS understanding of hospitality!

We are wandering strangers who come upon a community in the middle of our personal deserts, tired, vulnerable and in need of care and protection.

When we arrive, we are taken in by the patriarch, by the father, by God who quickly summons his whole family, the faithful to come and gather round, meet us and listen to our story.

His heart overflowing, God extends his protection to us—and he would rather die than let harm come to us, yes, even sacrificing…wait for it! Even if it means sacrificing his only son to protect and save us!

Can you see the gospel message?

HOSPITALITY DOESN'T HAVE TO BE THE PREPARATION OF a ten-course banquet, using the expensive china and complimented by music and dancing. Hospitality doesn't require us to protect someone at the cost of our own life, or the lives of any of our sons or daughters.

However, godly hospitality *does* mean we can make one more Facetime call after a long day of video calls so that friend of ours—you know, the one who lives by themselves and now works from home too—knows they are remembered and not alone.

Godly hospitality *does* mean that it is not too difficult to throw an extra burger or two on the grill and invite over the neighbor from across the street—you know, the one that we wave to each morning.

Godly hospitality *does* mean we will, in fact write and send that note, send that text message or email; that we will make that call rather than reflect on how good it would be, then falsely reassure ourselves that we'll "get to it later."

Godly hospitality *does* mean baking some cookies (or just buying some, and putting a few on a plate) and bringing them to that lonely neighbor two doors down who doesn't care whether or not they are fresh out of the oven, but only want to be dignified with the banter of idle conversation.

Godly hospitality *does* mean (and this is a tough one for me personally), letting someone merge in front of me on my commute without wishing the curse of a thousand plagues upon them—because the extra two seconds that I lost will clearly ruin my life!

Godly hospitality *does* mean complimenting that parent on how polite and respectful their child is being (this has led to more than one tearful conversation and expression of gratitude—let's face it, such parents of civil conviction are swimming upstream).

Godly hospitality *does* mean engaging someone in a conversation rather than simply looking at our phones. I have made it a point when appropriate to ask people with tattoos to tell me the story behind the ink. I have lost track of how many interesting and inspiring stories I've been privy to, simply because I asked and listened.

Would you agree that the Bedouin and biblical idea of hospitality are certainly better, easier, and yet far more dignifying; more loving and sacrificial than that of Martha Stewart? Would you agree that the Bedouin and biblical idea of hospitality better reflects the heart of Jesus and, when we have such a heart, by entertaining strangers we meet divinity?

If so, since this passage is about Jesus' disciples asking him how to pray, perhaps the best way to end this chapter is to pray the prayer He taught them to pray, saying:

> *Our father in heaven,*
> *Hallowed be your name.*
> *Your kingdom come,*
> *Your will be done*
> *on earth as it is in heaven.*
> *Give us this day, our daily bread.*
> *Forgive us our sins,*
> *as we forgive those who sin against us.*
> *Save us from the time of trouble*
> *and deliver us from evil,*
> *For yours is the kingdom,*
> *the power and glory*
> *forever.*
> *Amen.*

CHAPTER 7

Walk to the Cross—God Gave Us the Finger

(John 8)

remember the autumn day when I realized that the game of chess and disciplining my elementary-aged daughter were quite similar. While I don't recall the exact circumstances, I remember that I was the fortunate one to stay home with our older daughter who had been grounded for the day. As the mediator of justice, my mission was clear: be certain our convict-in-training remained inside the house without access to electronics and then, once her sentence was served, help transition her back to civil society.

Straightforward.

Simple.

I envisioned a quiet day where I could initially catch up on some articles that I'd been meaning to read and later, watch my favorite English Premier League team take on their cross-town rivals. With expectations set, I curled up in my wing back chair right between the window and the fireplace, inhaled deeply the aroma of fresh coffee brewing, and contentedly began to read the first article. I had not gotten halfway through the third paragraph when I heard the distant, muffled laughter of our daughter. Laying my magazine aside, I quietly rose from my chair and followed the sound to the foyer at the front of the house where, through the closed front door, I could hear the conversation my daughter was having with her imaginary playmate!

I couldn't believe it! In less than thirty minutes after I had been left in charge of the family prison, my jailbird was playing outside on the front porch—in direct violation of her grounding!

Flinging open the door, I brought an abrupt end to my daughter's laughter and conversation, replacing it instead with an awkward moment with the two of us staring at one another with looks that incredulously demanded an explanation of the other's intrusion. Finally breaking the silence, I demanded, "What do you think you are doing outside? You do remember that you're grounded, right?"

As if realizing the misunderstanding, my daughter smiled, and with the breeze gently blowing through her hair, reassuringly responded, "Dad, it's okay. I'm not outside. I'm on the porch."

My initial impulse was to point out the illogic of her statement, namely, that for an individual to legitimately be on the front porch, he or she would need to open and pass through a doorway which, to my way of thinking, delineates inside from outside. However, wanting to return as quickly as possible to the solitude of my wing back chair, I opted instead to further clarify for her what I meant by being "outside."

Now, I sense an obligation to tell you: I am no fool. I even have an advanced degree. And I was fully aware that our house had a deck in the back that could also be accessed through a door. So, given my daughter's rather loose definitions of *inside* and *outside*, coupled with my foresight and thoroughness, I looked directly at my daughter and said, "Just so we are clear: outside includes anything that entails you going through a door, window or vent to access any form or structure that is attached to the house, including, but not limited to, the front porch, back deck, rooftop or crawlspace. *Do you understand?*"

Reluctantly, she nodded and, after my persistently beckoning her to do so, walked reluctantly back *inside* the house from the *outside*.

Assured that a new level of communication and understanding had been achieved, I returned to my wing back chair and continued reading. Twenty minutes later, as I was getting up for a second cup of coffee, I again heard her muffled laughter, but this time coming from downstairs. I once again found myself following the sound, to the lower level and to the door that led to our attached garage. This time, I decided to slowly open the door and, peeking through the opening, observed my prisoner riding her bike in tight little circles in the empty garage bay, laughing and talking yet again to her imaginary friend (clearly, this friend was a bad influence). As she completed her loop, I came into view which motivated her to slam on her brakes, end her conversation, and once again stare at me as if to say, "Can I help you with something?"

I confess, for a moment, I felt like I was the one intruding and needed to apologize!

Deciding the best course of action was to wrest back control of the situation for the second time in less than an hour, I asked her (with more emphasis this time), *"What do you think you're doing?"*

Then it happened! It was a moment of pure, clear communication with absolutely no misunderstanding. It was a moment where the full breadth of what was transpiring between us revealed itself without a word spoken. Her smile and feigned innocence asked, "Whatever do you mean, dear Father?"

My intense, wordless gaze declared "You don't fool me. I know what you're doing!"

"Jesus returned to the Mount of Olives, but early the next morning he was back again at the Temple. A crowd soon gathered, and he sat down and taught them. As he was speaking, the teachers of the religious law and the Pharisees brought a woman who had been caught in the act of adultery. They put her in front of the crowd." (John 8:1-3, NLT)

One can immediately sense that something is off about this situation because of the very public way in which the religious leaders were accusing this woman. Within Jewish law there were proper channels to bring accusations against someone, channels that were more discrete and would have preserved some of the woman's dignity and humanity, regardless of what she was being accused. For some reason, however, these teachers of the law and Pharisees, who should have known better, decided a public spectacle was warranted, and the woman's dignity and humanity were of secondary concern. These devout followers of God chose instead to wield the greatest weapon of self-righteousness: the weapon of shame.

"'Teacher,' they said to Jesus, 'this woman was caught in the act of adultery. The law of Moses says to stone

her. What do you say?"' (John 8:4-5, NLT)

They were referring to two passages in the Torah, Leviticus 20:10 and Deuteronomy 22:22 which clearly state that she should be put to death. However, these learned and righteous leaders were conveniently leaving out an extremely important detail.

> *"If a man commits adultery with his neighbor's wife, both the man and the woman who have committed adultery must be put to death." (Leviticus 20:10, NLT)*

And,

> *"If a man is discovered committing adultery, both he and the woman must die. In this way, you will purge Israel of such evil." (Deuteronomy 22:22, NLT)*

The punishment for adultery afforded in these passages of scripture cannot be denied, but there is something amiss, something that is off between what the teachers of the law and Pharisees were demanding, and the woman who had been brought before Jesus in this very public and humiliating way.

Where was the man?

Where is the man who was *also* committing adultery and equally culpable under the law?

The law of the time was indeed clear that *both* the man and the woman were to be put to death. However, according to the passage, it seems the teachers of the law and Pharisees chose instead to bring only the woman before Jesus, and to do so in a most public and degrading manner.

Why?

The answer lies in the passage.

"[The teachers of the law and Pharisees] were trying to trap [Jesus] into saying something they could use against him..." (John 8:6a, NLT)

Under Roman law, only the Roman-appointed judge could authorize the death penalty, otherwise it was considered murder. Jesus did not have the authority under Roman law to sentence anybody to death. This was the trap. If Jesus answered that Jewish law was to be followed, he would be open to arrest and trial for inciting murder under Roman law. However, if Jesus answered that the woman should be allowed to go free (despite the injustice of the male in the adulterous relationship not being present), he could be accused of not upholding the Jewish law and being disobedient to God.

Take a moment, however, to fully grasp the scope of betrayal and depravity that is transpiring in this passage. The teachers of the law and Pharisees' hate and/or fear of Jesus is *so* great that they are willing to pervert the law and use this woman as a pawn, even willing to risk her being put to death in order to trap him! In the twisted, collective mind of these devout followers of God, this woman's public humiliation and potential death—not to mention the perversion and selective application of the very laws they are quoting–are somehow justified! Spiritualized barbarity, callous indifference, and a willingness to subvert the very purity and holiness they claim to be upholding, is sin at its most base and evil level.

Confronted with this trap, Jesus' response is unexpected.

"...but Jesus stopped down and wrote in the dust with his finger." (John 8:6b, NLT)

There has been much speculation on what Jesus was writing in the dust, ranging from the names of each accuser, to the sins that each had committed, to one of the two passages quoted above that contained the law. It could also have been doodles, tic-tac-toe or Sudoku! The truth is, we will never know.

Consider this, however.

By this time in the life of Jesus, word on the street was that this Jesus was engaging in some very messiah-like activities, begging the question, could he be the son of God? Jesus had obviously caused quite a stir, and so it would be reasonable to assume that anytime Jesus was publicly teaching and healing, people would be looking for indications of whether or not it was true.

Bearing this in mind, Jesus was the hands-on favorite of the people at the time to be the Messiah.

Confronted with this trap, Jesus stoops down and "...with his finger..." begins writing in the dust. To a devout Jew, I would suggest that God, writing with his finger, would conjure up some imagery that would bring relevant lessons from Israel's history into the present, imagery that would be relevant to the mob action with which Jesus was being confronted.

IN THE BOOK OF EXODUS, MOSES ASCENDS MT. SINAI eight times to meet with God, and on his sixth trip up the mountain, something crucial happens. It is during this ascent that he receives the stone tablets, what we refer to as the Ten Commandments.

"Then the Lord said to Moses, 'Come up to me on the mountain. Stay there, and I will give you the tablets of stone on which I have inscribed the instructions and commands so you can teach the people.'" (Exodus 24:12, NLT)

A wide range of topics are covered in these instructions and commands, including how to build the tabernacle, the ark of the Covenant, the altar and the priestly garments. Then, right before Moses begins his descent, the scripture says…

*"When the Lord finished speaking with Moses on Mount Sinai, he gave him the two stone tablets inscribed with the terms of the Covenant, written by the **finger of God.**" (Exodus 31:18, NLT, emphasis added)*

The finger of God has written something, inscribed the instructions and commands that Moses is to now share with the emerging people of God waiting at the base of Mount Sinai. With his finger, God has composed a blueprint of what this relationship between him and the people he has just delivered from slavery in Egypt will look like. The finger of God has inscribed a critical path and framework that defines the parameters in which a healthy relationship between the God who saves—and the people he saved—can be cultivated and maintained.

Unfortunately, even as the finger of God is writing, the relationship is already being violated by the very people to which it is being written; those impatiently waiting at the foot of Mount Sinai whom God has just brought out of Egypt.

> "When the people saw how long it was taking Moses to come back down the mountain, they gathered around Aaron. 'Come on,' they said, 'make us some gods who can lead us. We don't know what happened to this fellow Moses, who brought us here from the land of Egypt.' So Aaron said, 'Take the gold rings from the ears of your wives and sons and daughters and bring them to me.' All the people took the gold rings from their ears and brought them to Aaron. Then Aaron took the gold, melted it down and molded it into the shape of a calf. When the people saw it, they exclaimed, 'O Israel, these are the gods who brought you out of the land of Egypt!'" *(Exodus 32:1-4, NLT)*

Even as the finger of God outlines and establishes a relationship, that very relationship is being compromised and violated.

> "The Lord told Moses, 'Quick! Go down the mountain! Your people whom you brought from the land of Egypt have corrupted themselves. How quickly they have turned away from the way I have commanded them to live!'" *(Exodus 32:7-8a, NLT)*

Even while God is working to establish a relationship, that relationship is simultaneously being violated by those who claim their devotion.

The finger of God writes to a people who are quick to sell out the very relationship and faith to which they claim to be so unwaveringly devoted.

In fact, this tragic chapter in the life of Israel is so important that Moses felt compelled to include it in the book of Deuteronomy, a book that is arguably his farewell discourse to the emerging people of Israel. Moses did not want the people of Israel to forget that, even as God was writing the contract that defined their relationship, they were already compromising and violating it.

Using similar imagery from Exodus, Moses in Deuteronomy writes...

> *"The Lord gave me the two tablets on which God had written with **his own finger** all the words he had spoken to you..." (Deuteronomy 9:10, NLT, emphasis added)*

In his farewell discourse Moses was imploring Israel, "Don't do it again! Don't sell out the very relationship to which you claim devotion, especially as God is working to restore it!"

In the frenzy of the moment, the teachers of the law and Pharisees dragged a humiliated woman into a public forum, indifferent to their hate-filled motivation and self-righteous perversion of the law and demanded an answer. Jesus does something unexpected but filled with poignant imagery.

> *"...but Jesus stopped down and wrote in the dust **with his finger**." (John 8:6b, NLT, emphasis added)*

The question is not what did Jesus write in the dust; rather, what comes to mind for the teachers of the law, the Pharisees and the devout Jew when the finger of God writes? Speculation already exists that Jesus may be the Messiah, so the symbolism of the finger of God writing should not be understated or missed. Jesus' life, message and ministry are about seeking to restore and define what a relationship with God now looks like and simultaneously, just like at Mount Sinai, that very relationship is being violated!

Without saying a word, it's as if Jesus is saying "You're doing it again!" With the simple, symbolic act of the finger of God writing, Jesus demonstrates to the teachers of the law and Pharisees that the very relationship to which they claim devotion is once again being violated even as it is being reestablished. In short, Israel's past—and Moses' departing warning to remember—come roaring into the present as the devout and faithful violate their relationship with God by spiritualizing and justifying the denigration and sacrifice of this woman to satiate their hate of Jesus.

The passage goes on to relate that, at first, they don't make the connection because the teachers of the law and Pharisees demand an answer to their question. So, Jesus goes on to say…

> *"All right, but let the one who has never sinned throw the first stone!' Then he stooped down again and wrote in the dust." (John 8:7-8, NLT)*

Once again, Jesus is speaking without saying a word. Once again, with this simple action of writing in the dust, he seeks to conjure up the image of the finger of God writing about a relationship that is being violated.

Embedded in Jesus' action and its symbolism you can almost hear Jesus saying, "I see you. I know what you're doing! Do NOT be like your ancestors. Don't violate the very relationship I am literally, right here and now, trying to reestablish!"

By connecting their immediate action to those of their ancestors, Jesus pivots the moment to highlight what is truly unfolding, namely that these teachers and Pharisees are selling out their faith and the very relationship that, through the life and ministry of Jesus, God is seeking to restore.

It appears that they finally get it, because the passage next relates that…

"When the accusers heard this, they slipped away one by one…" (John 8:9a, NLT)

Why?

Because they know that the last time the finger of God wrote something, it was about their relationship to him and how they violated it before it could even be established. They know how Moses had to ascend Mount Sinai a seventh time, only this time to plead with God on behalf of those that had so quickly sold out their faith and relationship to him for a golden calf.

"Then the Lord said, 'I have seen how stubborn and rebellious these people are. Now leave me alone so my fierce anger can blaze against them, and I will destroy them. Then I will make you, Moses, into a great nation.'" (Exodus 32:9-10, NLT)

So, it would appear that on three different occasions in scripture, God and Jesus have given someone the finger, and each time it was an admonition to not sell out one's faith and relationship with God even as God is working to establish and/or restore it.

What does the passage say happens next?

"Then Jesus stood up again and said to the woman, 'Where are your accusers? Didn't even one of them condemn you?' 'No, Lord,' she said. And Jesus said, 'Neither do I.'" (John 8:10-11a, NLT)

With the devout and faithful accusers gone, the passage seems to imply that only Jesus, the woman, and a smaller, stunned crowd remain. I can visualize the image of Jesus, oblivious to those who remain, looking deeply and compassionately into the eyes of the woman. I can picture the woman slowly realizing that she is not going to die, and a shared, silent moment of pure communication and understanding passing between the two of them.

And, in the stunned quiet of the moment, we see the essence of what it means to be in relationship with God. Only moments before, the relationship between God and those who proclaimed to be most devout, learned, and righteous was about to be mocked, denigrated, and betrayed through the unjust stoning and death of a woman for the sole purpose of entrapping someone whom they hated.

Let me take a quick moment to address what some of you are bursting at the seams to call me out on (you know who you are, and you know that I'm right!). You want to shout from the rooftops "Wait! You've left out the most important words of the passage!"

> *"Then Jesus stood up again and said to the woman, 'Where are your accusers? Didn't even one of them condemn you?' 'No, Lord,' she said. And Jesus said, 'Neither do I. Go and sin no more.'" (John 8:10-11, NLT)*

"Go and sin no more." I am fully aware that I left those words out and did so intentionally, because I didn't want the main point of the passage to be subverted.

You see, one interpretation puts the emphasis on restoring a relationship with God, a relationship that we are much too quick to sell out due to our own self-righteousness and spiritual arrogance in pursuit self-interest. Another interpretation puts the emphasis on sin and the avoidance of punishment.

The former interpretation reflects the consistent nature and ministry of Jesus rooted in love, grace, inclusion, restoration, healing and hope. The latter interpretation, I would suggest, ultimately leads to the spiritualization of a heart and disposition that ends in worshipping a golden calf at the base of Mount Sinai or spiritualizing the unjust dragging and shaming of a woman in public in order to entrap a perceived enemy or threat.

As with my elementary-aged jailbird, there exists between Jesus and us a moment of pure, clear communication with absolutely no misunderstanding; a moment where the full breadth of what is transpiring between us is revealed without a spoken word. Like my pint-sized parolee, our naïve or willful innocence does not deflect the Father's convicting gaze that says, "You don't fool me. I know what you're doing."

Do NOT miss this: God, through Jesus, is seeking to reestablish relationship with all humanity!

Do NOT miss this: God, through Jesus, warns us yet again of our ability to declare our commitment to the relationship while simultaneously violating it.

Do NOT miss this: God, through Jesus, calls out the spiritualization and justification of any action that demeans, degrades, divides, diminishes, or denigrates anyone.

Do NOT miss this: God, through Jesus, calls out our blind fear and need for control; control that results in the affirmation or silent complicity to *any* system, action, or elected individual that acts in ways contrary to the very faith and relationship to which we declare fidelity.

Do NOT miss this: God, through Jesus, calls out a heart so calloused or misled as to subvert justice, promote indifference to the vulnerable or suffering, or twist biblical truth in such a way that its default is exclusion versus inclusion.

Do NOT make the same mistake of our ancestors of faith.

Do NOT ignore Jesus, kneeling once again; the finger of God writing in the dust of callous indifference and calling out a willingness to subvert the very purity that followers of Christ claim to uphold.

Do NOT make God give you, give us the finger again.

CHAPTER 8

Walk to the Cross—The Head of the Betrayer

(John 13)

As I settled into my aisle seat on the flight from Houston, Texas to Quito, Ecuador, I quickly glanced at the gentleman with whom I'd be sharing a row for the next five hours, nodded a greeting and buckled up. As I pulled out an in-flight magazine and began paging through it, I glanced toward the front of the plane and noticed two Immigration officers talking with a flight attendant. I also noted that my seat companion was leaning forward too, watching the group whose interest now seemed to focus on a clipboard that held some sort of list.

I looked over at him and said, "This could be interesting."

"I've flown to Quito quite a bit," he replied. "And I have never seen Immigration officers on a plane."

"Maybe the cartel has fallen on hard times." I quipped. "I hear it's cheaper to get to Bogota via Quito if you have the time."

He smiled and said, "Maybe there's a drug dealer or two on the plane."

Todd Slechta

We politely laughed at each other's wit just as the Immigration officers began walking down the aisle toward the back of the plane. As they made their way, I looked at my seat companion and jokingly said, "It looks like they know you're here."

The plane gradually grew more and more quiet as the passengers realized that these officers were looking for someone specific and, to be honest, there was a slight buzz of excitement as people began to wonder if they were going to see a real life take-down of a Columbian drug lord!

The first officer passed my seat, then stopped and turned around. I looked up at the second officer who had been following, but who had stopped at the row just in front of mine. I watched him check the aisle number against the paper he held in his hand, and then he looked straight down at me and asked, "Are you Mr. Slechta?"

To say I was surprised would be quite an understatement. I couldn't help noticing that my seat mate, who had earlier been joking around with me, was now conspicuously trying to use his body language to demonstrate that he did not know me in any way! Other passengers were whispering to one another and, if they were honest, were probably a little disappointed because my blonde hair and blue eyes didn't fit their profile of a Columbian drug lord.

"I am." I managed to answer.

"Will you come with us please?" he said, and then added, "And grab any carry-on luggage you may have."

At that moment, the situation began to sink in, and I realized that this just got very serious. Being asked to bring along my carry-on bag meant I was not getting back on the plane!

After pulling my computer bag out of the overhead bin, I followed the first Immigration officer toward the front while the second fell into step behind me. My heart was racing as I tried to figure out what had happened, what mistake had been made—or worse, what tragedy had befallen my family that would warrant my being pulled off the plane! The professional smile and "Buh-bye" of the flight attendant felt like mockery as I stepped off the plane and continued my walk up the jetway and back to the terminal where I had been waiting to board only thirty minutes earlier!

Once we were in the waiting area and the door to the jetway was closed, only then did the officers turn to me and explain that they didn't know how I got through security, but my passport was expired. They went on to explain that they were afraid if I arrived in Ecuador, the authorities would only turn me away and place me on the next flight back to the United States. They grudgingly admitted that, since it was partially their error for letting me through, they felt the best alternative was to pull me from the flight so I could go to the State Department office in Houston and have my passport renewed. They went on to say that, as a courtesy, they had already booked me on the same flight the next day at no cost to me!

I was relieved, angry, grateful, embarrassed and, admittedly a little surly. "You scared the crap out of me!" I disclosed to the officers. "I was ready to confess to anything! The minute you asked me to confirm my name, this trip went from boring to incredibly serious!"

Not knowing what else could be said, they simply apologized, wished me well and went on their way—perhaps to more pressing international matters. Taking a moment to gather myself, I sat down in one of the chairs and took a minute to review how, in only a couple of short minutes, a routine day had pivoted so significantly.

On the trips that I led to Israel/Palestine, we regularly visited a place called Yad Hoshmona whose mission is to give a glimpse into the spiritual, physical, and agricultural world of the Jewish people in the land of the Bible. Through experiences planned for us to observe, we were introduced to customs surrounding life events, such as engagement and marriage rituals as well as seating customs at formal meals. On one occasion, we were given such a profound insight into the Passover meal that I had a moment like when the Immigration Officer said my name and asked me to follow him off the plane. The insight was so profound that I recall thinking to myself, "This just got really serious." Since then, I have not participated in the sacrament of communion in the same way, the experience being wonderfully vested with more depth and meaning than ever before.

As difficult as this may be to grasp, most marriages in biblical times were, for all intents and purposes, a contract between two families, unlike our familiar celebration of two individuals who have discovered one another and fallen in love. The fathers of the future bride and groom would negotiate the arrangement, most notably the amount and manner of payment of the bride's dowry. The dowry was the money or goods that a bride's family gave to her new husband and/or his family to assure that she was taken care of, should she survive her husband.

Once the fathers came to an agreement, they would take a cup of wine and each take a sip, formalizing the arrangement. Then, the father of the groom would hand the cup to his son who would take a sip, and he, in turn, would offer it to his potential fiancée, symbolically saying "I offer you my life." This was a pivotal moment because, in theory, the young woman could decline the proposal of marriage thereby nullifying the agreement between the families. I am under no illusion that the pressure against doing so was undoubtedly quite intense because, by the conclusion of the negotiations, this consulting of the bride-to-be was more ceremonial and a mere formality— much like the familiar wedding phrase, "who gives this bride?" In theory however, it remained a moment when the female *could* decline. But if she agreed, she would accept the offered cup of wine from her future fiancée, take a sip and symbolically indicate, "I accept your life, and offer you mine, as well."

In 1 Corinthians 11:23-25, we encounter Paul's words, words that still serve as part of the liturgy of most celebrations of the sacrament of communion. Paul relates that he passes on to us, the readers, what he received…

> "…*from the Lord himself. On the night when he was betrayed, the Lord Jesus took some bread and gave thanks to God for it. Then he broke it in pieces and said, 'This is my body, which is given for you. Do this in remembrance of me.' In the same we, he took the cup of wine after supper, saying, 'This cup is the new covenant between God and his people—an agreement confirmed with my blood. Do this in remembrance of me as often as you drink it.'" (1 Corinthians 11:23-25, NLT)*

In the liturgy of most Passover celebrations, four cups are used to symbolize various aspects of the historical deliverance of the Hebrew people from slavery in Egypt. The third cup is called the Cup of Redemption, the cup that symbolizes God setting things right. The drinking of this cup comes *after* dinner, so when Paul says in verse 25 that Jesus took "…the cup of wine after supper…," every devout Jew would know that this was the cup to which he was referring.

Depending on the number that gathered together to celebrate Passover, it was not uncommon that every guest would have one symbolic cup from which they would drink at the four appropriate times in the liturgy. The patriarch would have four distinct cups that he would lift for all to view as he recited the liturgy and the family and guests would join at the appropriate times taking sips from their single symbolic cup.

I find it interesting that in the Gospel of Matthew, arguably the most Jewish of all the gospels, it says:

> *"And he took a cup of wine and gave thanks to God for it. He gave it to them and said, 'Each of you drink from it...'" (Matthew 26:27, NLT)*

I visualize the image of Jesus, giving thanks for the cup as the liturgy of Passover requires, taking a sip and then, instead of waiting for the disciples to each take a drink from their symbolic cups, he turns to one of the disciples and offers the cup from which he'd just drank. I wonder if, in doing so, it conjured up images of the engagement ritual, in a sense Jesus turning to his disciples and saying, "I offer you my life." And, as was the case with the bride to be, the disciple had a choice to say no, or to accept the cup, take a sip and in essence say, "I accept your life and offer you mine, as well."

I wonder if this ever-so-slight break from the liturgy, this subtle blending of Passover liturgy and engagement custom caused them to pause because a typically mundane ritual suddenly became incredibly serious, vesting the moment with new depth and understanding. There was, after all, a lot of symbolism to the engagement customs of the time that would provide a fertile context.

For example, the young groom-to-be most likely did not

have a home himself, typically occupying a room or place in his father's house on the family compound.

As custom would have it, once the arrangement was made between the two families, the groom-to-be would leave his fiancée with her family, return to his family compound and begin building and preparing a separate room for his future wife. You can imagine how anxious the son would be to get this addition completed because, once it was ready, he could return for his fiancée, be married and they could begin their life together.

This imagery is captured by Jesus in John 14:1-4 when, following the disturbing conversation regarding someone who will betray him, he seeks to reassure his disciples saying:

> *"Don't let your hearts be troubled. Trust in God, and trust also in me. There is more than enough room in my Father's home. If this were not so, would I have told you that I'm going to prepare a place for you? When everything is ready, I will*

come and get you, so that you will always be with me where I am. And you know the way to where I am going." (John 14:1-4, NLT)

Can you visualize the image of an impatient son working on the addition to the home, calling his dad to check if it is ready and sign off on it, and being so dismayed when his father tells him to fix some minor error or oversight in his new addition? Then, quickly making the improvements— again calling for his dad to check on the work—all the while waiting eagerly for the moment when his father would declare the addition ready to receive his son's fiancée. That day was a day of great celebration, because the groom-to-be would gather his family and friends and, in a procession filled with singing, dancing and music, return to the home of his fiancée, gather her back to their new home, complete the marriage ceremony, and begin the new life together as a married couple.

The richness of the customs surrounding engagement and marriage during biblical times cannot be understated or overlooked. To do so would mean to miss significant depth and understanding.

Adding as well to the depth and understanding of communion, on another experience at Yad Hoshmona, a teacher gave some wonderful insight into the seating customs in 1st century Palestine. Tables were low to the ground and did not require chairs, so diners ate in a crisscross or reclined position. Additionally, tables typically were arranged in the shape of a "U" (see below):

It was customary to recline or rest on one's left elbow (see arrow above) and use your right hand to reach for food and eat. Following dinner, as the meal was settling, diners would recline and lay their heads on the chest of the person to their left, like an early version of what evolved into the popular youth ministry icebreaker, the Ha-Ha game[12]. In today's culture, this would undoubtedly be uncomfortable for most and for many, even viewed as an incredible violation of personal space—but

12. If you are unfamiliar with this popular icebreaker, go to YouTube and search for "How to Play the Ha-Ha Game." Enjoy and, you're welcome.

not so in biblical times. In fact, if the person on whom one's head was reclined asked for another bite of food, the reclining individual would simply retrieve what was asked, reach over his shoulder and hand it to the individual.

Another interesting cultural aspect regarding seating arrangements was that one's status was indicated by where one sat. When standing at the open end of the "U," the table to the left was considered the more prestigious place, where the more important guests were seated because the host of the meal and guest of honor sat very nearby. The host typically sat in the second position (indicated by the arrow below), allowing for a guest to sit on either side of him, and the position to the host's left was generally reserved for the guest of honor, then the next person of status sat on the right side, or at the right hand of the host.

This seating custom is at play in the background of Matthew 20:20-21, when the mother of James and John asks Jesus to allow her two sons to sit in the places of honor next to him.

"Then the mother of James and John, the sons of Zebedee, came to Jesus with her sons. She knelt respectfully

to ask a favor. 'What is your request?' he asked. She replied, 'In your Kingdom, please let my two sons sit in places of honor next to you, one on your right and the other on your left.'" (Matthew 20:20-21, NLT)

We know that Jesus was the host for the Passover meal, so it is easy to deduce that Jesus was reclined in the host position, second from the end on the left side of the table.

"One of them, the disciple whom Jesus loved, was reclining next to him." (John 3:23, NLT)

John's gospel is clear that it was he who was reclining next to Jesus in one of the two positions of honor, designated #1 and #3 in the picture below.

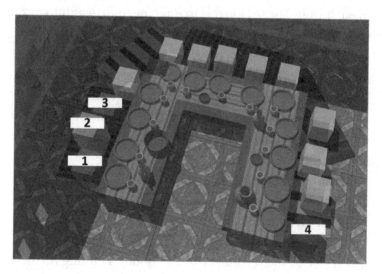

With a little more deduction, not only do we find a second reference to the fact that John was seated in one of the two positions next to Jesus, but we can even determine that he was positioned to Jesus' right (position #1).

> *"Now Jesus was deeply troubled, and he exclaimed, 'I tell you the truth, one of you will betray me!' The disciples looked at each other, wondering whom he could mean. The disciple Jesus loved was sitting next to Jesus at the table. Simon Peter motioned to him to ask, "Who's he talking about?' So that disciple leaned over to Jesus and asked, 'Lord, who is it?'" (John 13:21-24, NLT)*

Remember: following a meal, it was common for the guests to relax, talk and share—much as we do today. When doing so in that era, they would lean backward and rest their head on the chest of the person to their left. In the context of this meal, it would be reasonable to imagine John, leaning over—which actually meant leaning *back* onto Jesus' chest to ask the question. This lends plausibility to the idea that he was sitting to Jesus' right at one of the two seats of honor, most likely where the second most important guest sat.

This begs the question, can we determine who might have been seated to Jesus' left, the seat traditionally reserved for the guest of honor?

According to Luke 9:28 and Mark 14:33 Jesus seemed to have an inner circle of disciples, Peter, James and John. Since we know where John was seated, logically one might assume that one of the other inner circle, Peter or James was seated at the secondary seat of honor. Lending further plausibility to it being one of these two is the fact that we know that Jesus sent Peter and John ahead to prepare for the Passover Meal (Luke 22:8). Since they helped with the preparation and John was already at the right hand of Jesus, we can fairly assume that Peter would be on the left-hand side of Jesus as the guest of honor.

Unfortunately, Peter was not invited to that seat because, in John 13:24, when Jesus announced that someone would betray him, we know that Peter had to motion to get John's attention before prompting him to ask Jesus who was the betrayer. This would mean that Peter had to have been positioned in such a way that, from a reclining position, he could make eye contact with John. More than likely, this would place Peter somewhere in a position opposite John, most likely somewhere at the table on the right-hand side, the least desirable seats.

This setting grows even more interesting because we also know that, before reclining to eat, it was customary at formal meals to wash the guests' feet, beginning with the seats of honor on the left-hand side, then working one's way around to the final position on the far right. In John's account of Jesus washing the disciples' feet, Peter appears to be the last to have his feet washed. This detail matters because it would mean that Peter was likely seated in the final position on the far-right side, in the very last position (see arrow below).

The last seat on the far-right side was considered the servant seat, for the individual charged with assuring that the meal was properly served. This individual also had the responsibility of washing the dusty feet of the guests before the meal started, so Peter was most definitely *not* seated as the guest of honor! One could imagine that Peter was not pleased with his placement at the table (especially since John, who helped prepare the meal, had been invited to sit at Jesus' right hand)!

Throughout the Gospels we see that Peter could sometimes be a bit impulsive, and this may have been one of those instances. If in fact this is where Peter was seated, then it was his job to wash the feet of the guests *before* dinner. He would first wash the feet of the guest of honor, then the guest on the host's right-hand side (in this instance, John), then the host (Jesus), before working his way around the table until all the guests' feet were cleaned. Finally, he would wash his own feet and the meal would could begin.

However, apparently this washing of feet was not being done by anyone, specifically Peter, because according to John:

> *It was time for supper,…So [Jesus] got up from the table, took off his robe, wrapped a towel around his waist, and poured water into a basin. Then he began to wash the disciples' feet, drying them with the towel he had around him" One of them, the disciple whom Jesus loved, was reclining next to him."* (John 13:1a, 4-5, NLT)

Put yourself in Peter's place for a moment and imagine sitting in the last seat: the servant seat. Then picture Jesus, your Rabbi and host of the dinner, slowly working his way around the table, and humbly doing the servant's task of washing the feet of the guests. Jesus was doing the task that had been asked of *you*, but which, for whatever reason, you chose not to accept. Closer and closer Jesus comes until he arrives at the last seat—your seat—the servant seat. Can you imagine the level of embarrassment, shame and conviction you would feel?

Apparently, that is how Peter must have felt, because his response when Jesus arrives at his seat is quite revealing. Out of shame, Peter simply wants Jesus to pass him by, but Jesus persists. Peter then responds—and you can almost hear his broken and repentant heart.

> *"When Jesus came to Simon Peter, Peter said to him, 'Lord, are you going to wash my feet?'*
>
> *Jesus replied, 'You don't understand now what I am doing, but someday you will.'*
>
> *'No,' Peter protested, 'you will never ever wash my feet!'*
>
> *Jesus replied, 'Unless I wash you, you won't belong to me.'*
>
> *Simon Peter exclaimed, 'Then wash my hands and head as well, Lord, not just my feet!'" (John 13:6-9, NLT)*

Before we determine who was sitting in the seat of the guest of honor, it is important to note that, during the Passover Meal, it was customary for the host to dip a piece of bread into the main meat course (called the sop) and, reaching over his shoulder, offer it to the Guest of Honor. Knowing that, let's allow Jesus to tell us who was seated to his left and the honored guest.

> *"Now Jesus was deeply troubled, and he exclaimed, 'I tell you the truth, one of you will betray me!'*

The disciples looked at each other, wondering whom he could mean. The disciple Jesus loved was sitting next to Jesus at the table. Simon Peter motioned to him to ask, 'Who's he talking about?' So that disciple leaned over to Jesus and asked, 'Lord, who is it?'

Jesus responded, 'It is the one to whom I give the bread I dip in the bowl.' And when he had dipped it, he gave it to Judas, son of Simon Iscariot."

(John 13:21-26, NLT)

Let that sink in for a moment.

Judas, son of Simon Iscariot.

Judas Iscariot.

The guest of honor at the last supper was Judas, the one who betrays Jesus.

Though aware of Judas' planned betrayal, a betrayal that would set off a sequence of events culminating in his humiliating and protracted suffering on the cross, Jesus chooses to honor his betrayer!

Have you truly let that reality sink into your brain yet?!

Jesus washes the feet of his betrayer!

Jesus, with the agony of the cross before him, at the end of the meal reclines and lays his head on the chest of the one who will betray him.

Jesus—after the meal and whenever there was a lull in the conversation—literally hears the heartbeat of his betrayer.

Jesus washes the feet of those we are supposed to wash.

Are the feet a different color than mine? A servant washes them anyway.

Are the feet those of a refugee here illegally? A servant washes them anyway.

Are the feet those of someone of a different faith? A servant washes them anyway.

Are the feet those of a different sexual orientation? A servant washes them anyway.

Are the feet physically disfigured? A servant washes them anyway.

Are the feet of those who wrestle with mental health? A servant washes them anyway.

Are the feet of someone who betrays you? A servant washes them anyway.

As I imagine Jesus reclining his head on the chest of Judas Iscariot, the liturgy of my church's communion strikes me in a different, more powerful and intimate way.

> *"Come to this sacred table, not because you must, but because you may; come to testify not that you are righteous, but that you sincerely love our Lord Jesus Christ and desire to be his true disciples; come not because you are strong, but because you are weak; not because you have any claim on the grace of God, but because in your frailty and sin you stand in constant need of his mercy and help; come not to express an opinion, but to seek his presence and pray for his spirit."*[13]

13. *The Covenant Book of Worship*, Covenant Publications, Chicago, IL, 2003, pg. 162

Come, not because we must, but because we may.

Come, not because we have a right to do so, but because we may.

Come, not to make a statement of our righteousness, but because we may.

Come, messy and broken, because we may.

Come, for such is the heart of the Host of the meal, that he would honor his betrayer and wash his feet.

Communion will always remain an incredibly serious event for me because, as the cup is offered, I now hear Jesus saying "Todd, I offer you my life."

And, in a moment, I realize that this just got incredibly serious. I must consciously declare yet again, "Jesus, I accept your life, and offer you mine, as well."

CHAPTER 9

Walk to the Cross—Being Holy, Being Crushed

(Mark 14)

D espite my intrigue with technology and its advances, I still enjoy the feel of a book in my hands (and don't even get me started on how much I enjoy locally owned bookstores). Throw in the smell of freshly brewed coffee on an overcast, drizzly day, and I just may hear a choir of angels singing! Don't get me wrong: because I travel a lot, I rely heavily on my iPad and Kindle because they allow me to bring four or five books on one device, saving the weight and space. But whenever practical, I much prefer to hold a book in my hands and turn its pages! My family and friends still give me books or gift cards to bookstores as presents.

One particular book, given to me about twenty years ago, is a volume that I still treasure entitled *Children's Letters to God*.[14] If you haven't read it yet, I encourage you to get a copy. A compilation of short, two or three sentence

---

14.   Hample, Stuart & Marshall, Eric, *Children's Letters to God*, Workman Publishing, NY, 1991.

letters by children to God, this book clarifies their innocent simplicity as simultaneously endearing and incisive.

A few of my personal favorites:

"We read Thomas Edison made light. But in Sunday School they said you did it. So I bet he stole your idea."
—Donna

"Dear God, Thank you for the baby brother but what I prayed for was a puppy." —Joyce

"Dear God, Maybe Cain and Abel would not kill each other so much if they had their own rooms. It works with my brother." —Larry

"Dear God, It is great the way you always get the stars in the right places." —Jeff

"Dear God, Did you mean for the giraffe to look like that or was it an accident."—Norma

Being a Coloradan at heart however, one of my favorite letters is:

"Dear God, I didn't think orange went with purple until I saw the sunset you made on Tuesday. That was cool! —Eugene, 8 years old

Another biblical principle evident throughout scripture is this: faith is hindsight 20/20, moving from disorientation to orientation. This principle has been at work throughout my entire journey of faith and, on many occasions, when I have reminded myself that it is at work, I have been able to move through sentiments of confusion, frustration or disappointment by knowing that, on the other side, I will be surprised by how God was and is at work.

In the Garden of Gethsemane and prior to his crucifixion, scripture relates an episode of anguish that Jesus experiences. However, before we delve into the related scriptures, let's get our heads around a couple of relevant details that the Bible assumes you already know. First, we need to gain some rudimentary insight into how first century Jewish thought understood blood, learn a little about the olive oil industry, and finally, be more aware of the location of the Garden of Gethsemane. Once we do those three tasks, we will be able to say in the spirit of eight-year-old Eugene, "Dear God, I didn't think blood and oil went together, until Gethsemane. That was cool! Thanks!"

THERE IS AN OLD GOSPEL HYMN ENTITLED "ARE YOU *Washed in the Blood?*"[15], whose lyrics include:

> *Have you been to Jesus for the cleansing power?*
> *Are you washed in the blood of the Lamb?*
> *Are you fully trusting in His grace this hour?*
> *Are you washed in the blood of the Lamb?*
> *Are you washed in the blood,*
> *In the soul-cleansing blood of the Lamb?*
> *Are your garments spotless? Are they white as snow?*
> *Are you washed in the blood of the Lamb?*

Have you ever tried to wipe up a significant amount of blood? For the record, I feel compelled to clarify that I don't have a lot of experience cleaning up significant amounts of blood, but a simple, disturbing YouTube search demonstrates how difficult

15. "Are You Washed in the Blood?", Elisha Hoffman, 1878.

it is (Word of advice? Delete your search history. It will save hours of awkward explanations to your now understandably paranoid partner!). In fact, blood doesn't *wash* anything. When you attempt to wipe it up without a special solution, all you do is spread it around, covering an even greater area with a thin layer of blood. Blood smears and covers. It doesn't wash.

So how exactly does one get *washed in the blood* because, practically-speaking, blood just gets all over us. Blood covers us.[16]

Against the pragmatic reality that blood smears and covers, comes this insightful passage that, understandably for many, is their life-verse:

> *"...for the life of the body is in its blood. I have given you the blood on the altar to purify you, making you right with the Lord. It is the blood, given in exchange for a life, that makes purification possible. That is why I have said to the people of Israel, 'You must never eat or drink blood—neither you nor the foreigners living among you.'"*
> *(Leviticus 17:11-12, NLT)*

It would be fair to say that, in Jesus' time, blood was understood to be viewed as not only life-sustaining, but life-giving. As this passage indicates, the "...life of the body is in its blood..." Perhaps this understanding is at work in Acts 15:20 at the Council of Jerusalem as leaders sought to understand and address the many new questions that emerged following the conversion of so many Gentiles to the faith. This passage also indicates that blood was understood to have a redemp-

---

16. I am cognizant of the symbolism that is at play in this hymn, speaking toward the blood of the Lamb, Jesus Christ *washing away* our sin. However, constricting the idea solely to this one aspect of the symbolism, we miss a greater and deeper meaning.

tive aspect, having the ability to make things "...right with the Lord." It is from this idea, from the redemptive aspect of sacrificial blood that modern Protestant and evangelical Christians have gained meaning from what we understand to be Jesus' sacrificial and redemptive actions on the cross.

It is reasonable to deduce that, to the first century Jewish way of thinking, blood in the physical sense smears—it covers things and, simultaneously in the spiritual sense—grants new life and is life-giving.

Following the Last Supper, Scripture says that Jesus went to pray in an olive grove located still today just outside the Old City of Jerusalem (the Mount of Olives). In the Gospel of Mark, Chapter 14, this olive grove was called Gethsemane, most likely derived from the Aramaic word "gat semãnê," which means "olive press," indicating that, if not during the time of Jesus, certainly in ancient times, a mill of some sort existed there.

Let's invest a moment in understanding a little more about the business of olive farmers. Crushing olives in order to produce olive oil was a significant industry in biblical Palestine, and there were two main methods for extracting it. In the pictures below, one such method is illustrated:

Olives were poured into the basin in which sat a millstone. A wooden beam was slid into the millstone and secured. Then a donkey (or a couple of men) would push on the beam, in turn rolling the millstone in a slow circle around the basin, rolling over and crushing the ripe olives into a pulp. The oil from these crushed olives would flow into channels that drained into vats. The oil was then transferred into various containers for sale, based on quality and size.

A second method for crushing and collecting olive oil is demonstrated in following picture:

This method leveraged the idea of a fulcrum. Baskets of ripe olives were stacked upon one another and then a beam was strategically laid across the baskets (see arrow above). Then, heavy stones were placed in such a way that their gradual weight pulled down on the beam which in turn pressed down on the stack of baskets of olives, crushing them and squeezing out the olive oil. Here too, the oil ran into a pit where it was then collected into containers for sale, based on quality and size.

This last method of extraction produced three distinct grades, or qualities, of oil. With the weight of the first stone came the initial *squeeze* of the ripe olives, the first drops, and this olive oil was the purest, meaning that it had the least amount of pulp and therefore the highest quality. These first few drops were precious and pure, and therefore set apart for the religious purposes of anointing and purifying. A second *squeeze* of the ripe olives came by adding another stone to the weight of the first. This second grade of olive oil, while not as pure as the initial drops, was still of high quality and utilized primarily for cooking and food preparation. Finally, a third stone could be added to the collective weight of the first two giving a final *squeeze* to the ripe olives. This produced the lowest grade of olive oil and was sold primarily as a lubricant for every day, common use (think: a biblical brand of WD40!).

By way of summary, one could reasonably say that in first century, biblical Palestine, the understanding that blood both covers and grants life co-existed and mingled with the idea that the first drops of olive oil were sacred, to be used for the holy purposes of anointing and purifying.

Now, the location of the Garden of Gethsemane on the Mount of Olives is informative. The following photo was taken from the Garden of Gethsemane looking west, over the Kidron valley toward the city of Jerusalem.

From this vantage point, Jesus and his disciples would have clearly been able to see the Temple in all its glory (where the iconic Dome of the Rock stands today). In the distance, just to right of the gold dome, one can make out two grey domes, one light and one dark (see arrow above). This is the traditionally accepted site of Calvary on which the Church of the Holy Sepulcher now stands. Tradition holds that, on this site, the crucifixion of Jesus took place.

If one were to crest the Mount of Olives and look to the east, one would find the desolate region of the Judean wilderness. As seen in the picture below, in Jesus' time it was a desolate area where few resided:

To the west, was the Temple and ultimately the place where Jesus was crucified. To the east, desolate wilderness. I'm always struck by the notion that, knowing what lay before him, Jesus could have easily disappeared into the wilderness and no one would have been the wiser. He would simply have been another man claiming to be the Messiah, but ultimately amounting to nothing. He could have gone back to his life as an obscure son of a carpenter content with what his ministry to date had accomplished.

But he didn't.

Instead, according to the Gospel of Mark we read...

> "They went to the olive grove called Gethsemane, and Jesus said, 'Sit here while I go pray.' He took Peter, James, and John with him, and he became deeply troubled and distressed. He told them, 'My soul is crushed with grief to the point of death. Stay here and keep watch with me.'

121

He went on a little farther and fell to the ground. He prayed that, if it were possible, the awful hour awaiting him might pass him by. 'Abba, Father,' he cried out, 'everything is possible for you. Please take this cup of suffering away from me. Yet I want your will to be done, not mine.'" (Mark 14:32-36, NLT)

Jesus chooses not to take the easier option to disappear into the Judean wilderness to the East. Instead, with the Temple looming to the West and with Calvary laying just beyond—where his brutal crucifixion would take place—he instead chooses God's will over his own. In the Garden of Gethsemane, where the crushing of olives for their sacred oil was practiced every day, it seems appropriate that Jesus shares that his "...soul is *crushed* with grief" (14:34, emphasis added). The imagery of the weight of the stones being used to crush olives cannot be lost. As the olives were crushed under the weight of the stones, similarly, Jesus' soul was being crushed under the weight of the path before him. Perhaps here, in this moment we see a glimpse of the humanity of Jesus.

The Gospel of Luke adds an intriguing detail.

*"'Father, if you are willing, please take this cup of suffering away from me. Yet I want your will to be done, not mine.' Then an angel from heaven appeared and strengthened him. He prayed more fervently, and he was in such agony of spirit that his sweat fell to the ground like great **drops of blood**." (Luke 22:42-44, NLT, emphasis added)*

The first few precious drops of olive oil are the purest, used only for anointing and purifying.

Luke says that Jesus' sweat fell to the ground like great drops of blood, and blood both covers and gives life.

Though this verse from Luke is not found in some of the ancient manuscripts, the symbolism is intriguing.

We know that blood doesn't clean what it touches. Blood covers. Could it be that the blood of Jesus doesn't so much as cleanse us of our sin, but rather covers it so that God can't *see* it? To be clear, I don't think an omniscient God forgets, because omniscience precludes forgetfulness. By forgetting our sin, could it mean that, unlike us, unlike me, God can forget our sin in the sense that he is capable of not holding it against us, that it doesn't affect the way he engages and interacts with us moving forward?

We also know that those first few and precious drops of oil are used for anointing and purifying. Could it be that these first few precious drops of blood signify Jesus' anointing and purification in preparation for something? We know that blood gives life, so, could it be that Luke chose the metaphor of drops of blood to conjure up the image of life-giving blood, foreshadowing his redemptive act on the cross?

Maybe Luke was brilliantly providing a framework to which the disciples (and we) would later cling for understanding, namely that Jesus' blood on the cross covers sins so that God can't *see* them anymore, while simultaneously granting new life, as is the inherent nature of blood.

If that is true, then the words of Jesus strike with even greater poignancy and depth: "I want your will to be done, not mine."

Anointed and covered by God, in pursuit of "his will, not mine;" this is the disposition of the heart and action of a disciple of Jesus Christ.

Anointed and covered by God, in pursuit of his will, not mine; this is the sort of humble strength and quiet conviction of godly people that our culture and world desperately need and long for.

Anointed and covered by God, in pursuit of his will, not mine; this is the sort of selflessness that piqued the heart and souls of so many in the early church who chose a way of hardship in emulating Jesus.

Anointed and covered by God, in pursuit of his will, not mine; this is the source of courage that emboldens true disciples of Jesus to overcome fear, biases, prejudices, oppressive systems that impoverish, privilege, misogyny, and dangerous, silent indifference; the conditions of the heart that permit degradation and dehumanization of people groups.

Anointed and covered by God, in pursuit of his will, not mine, is why I cringe when, in today's cultural climate, someone calls me a Christian, because this designation has become so entwined with so many things that stand in stark contrast to what we see of Jesus in Gethsemane that, if I'm honest, I'm embarrassed to be associated with the term.

I do, however desire to emulate an anguishing, vulnerable savior in Gethsemane who, after a moment of struggle, being holy and being crushed, ultimately whispers, "I want your will to be done, not mine."

CHAPTER 10

Walk to the Cross—Forward to the Past

(Matthew 27)

Orthodox[17] Christian belief holds that Jesus Christ was and is—simultaneously—human and deity; 100% human and 100% divine.

"In the beginning the Word already existed. The Word was with God, and the Word was God. He existed in the beginning with God. God created everything through him, and nothing was created except through him. The Word gave life to everything that was created, and his life brought light to everyone.

So the Word became human and made his home among us. He was full of unfailing love and faithfulness.

---

17.   At its most simple definition, orthodox means *right thinking;* relating to, or conforming to the approved form of any doctrine, philosophy, ideology, etc... In this case, the generally agreed upon understanding within the majority Christendom (Catholic, Protestant, Orthodox, etc...) is that the *Word* in this passage is Jesus Christ.

*And we have seen his glory, the glory of the Father's one
and only Son." (Matthew John 1:1-5, 14, NLT)*

This is why the following passage is troublesome for many,
especially those exploring the reality of Jesus Christ as God:

> *"At noon, darkness fell across the whole land until
> three o'clock. At about three o'clock, Jesus called out
> in a loud voice, 'Eli, Eli, lema sabachthani?' which
> means 'My God, my God, why have you abandoned
> me?'" (Matthew 27:45-45, NLT)*

As someone who attends church regularly, I have heard
various pastors preach and teach on this passage at least
a dozen times and, in every instance, the lesson to be
gleaned is that we are gaining a rare glimpse into Jesus'
humanity. In general, the sermons have sought to highlight that what we see in this passage is Jesus, the man,
hanging on the cross in utter pain, shame and agony,
despairingly calling out to God, his Father. What we see
is Jesus experiencing hell on earth, experiencing She'ol,
the pit, the one place from which God willingly withholds
his presence thereby creating a sense of complete separa-
tion and isolation. What we see in this passage is Jesus
paralleling the suffering of Job and, like Job, Jesus cries
out, feeling as if God had abandoned him and also like
Job, despite feeling like it is God himself who is causing
the pain (Job 13:15)[18], Jesus refuses to give up hope or to
stop trusting God.

---

18. An alternate reading in the Masoretic Text reads *"God might kill me,
but I hope in him."*

My intent is not to detract from these insights, but rather, to enhance them because I agree that this passage does give a unique glimpse into Jesus the human.

However, we also know that Jesus was, and is Jewish. Jesus was, and is a Rabbi and teacher. So, it is reasonable to deduce that Jesus would think, speak and act like a Rabbi, even as he faced death.

In general terms, we North Americans are a product of western thinking, which means we tend to think linearly. To oversimplify and make the point, western thinking tends to emulate the formula:

$$A + B + C = D$$

It is linear, sequential and, speaking in general terms, why we believe on some visceral level that we arrive at D *only if* we first engage A, then B, then C. We believe in the value of systems, procedures and processes.

Remember, our cultural roots are in the Roman Empire, the empire that brought a system of roads and transportation, and a system of education that predominated our philosophy of public education through the mid-1970s. This is the empire that brought us a system of aqueducts and enhanced forms of government and law.[19] This empire had an incessant need to organize all things and has had (and still has) a profound influence on Christian faith because it is from the Western expression of Christianity that we derived (wait for it) *systematic*

---

19. For a hilarious introduction of the influence of Rome, please watch a two-minute scene from *Monty Python's the Life of Brian* by going to You-Tube and searching the phrase "what has Rome ever done for us." Once again, you're welcome!

theology, a way of accessing and *systematically* studying the nature of God and religious thought—the bane of most seminary students!

Lest you think I am overstating how pervasive is this linear, systematic way of thinking, let me ask you to recall the last time you visited the self-help section of a bookstore, in person or online. What a glorious time in which we live! We literally can find any number of books that outline the "three or four-easy-steps" to solving and/or accomplishing everything!

Three easy steps to…raising children.
Four easy steps to…divorce recovery.
Two easy steps to…financial independence.
And the list goes on and on.

If, however, you've ever tried to assemble *anything* from IKEA, you received a lesson on how life really works! Reality looks more like this:

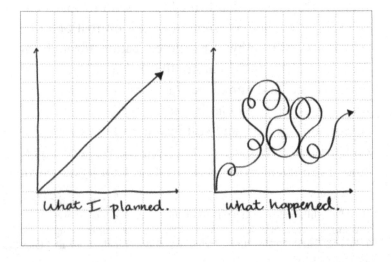

How many of us would ever suggest that raising children involves just three *easy* steps? If your experience was like ours, those steps we read about and prepared for in advance of the birth of our daughters were very effective–that is, until they were born! Then the steps weren't as *easy* as we were promised and, in some instances, completely unrealistic, because they didn't account for the fact that our children were human!

Seriously now, how easy are *any* steps to follow, regardless of how few or many, when it comes to recovering from a divorce? From the stories of friends who have walked that road, I know it is rarely clear and clean, that it is often two steps forward, three steps back, five steps forward before stumbling backward a step, then pausing while painfully garnering the courage to try another step forward.

Ask any recovering addict about the simplicity and ease of following the 12-step program. Please understand I don't want to sound critical of the program; it has obviously been beneficial to many, with incredible testimonies of human achievement and recovery. My point is simply that we are, more than we realize, a product and reflection of this western, linear, procedural form of thinking—and so, understandably, it is our natural, default position when approaching almost anything.

On the other end of the continuum, however, is what I will unfairly oversimply as an Eastern way of thought. I was introduced to the idea through various individuals who have influenced me throughout my life of faith, including an Eastern Orthodox bishop and a Talmud teacher. Eastern thinking differs significantly from West-

ern as it is more chiastic[20] in nature, tending more to
emulate the formula:

A B C **D** C B A

From this perspective, the emphasis lies at the center; at the
point labeled "D." The general idea depicted here is that events,
experiences and thought flow toward a moment, crest and
then proceed back down toward the beginning level. Perhaps a
better image would be that of a roller coaster as it races toward
the crest of a segment of track, incrementally losing momentum until it is almost at a crawl by the time it reaches the peak.
However, just enough momentum remains to ease the cars over
the crest, before again gaining forward momentum. Another
image would be the way an ocean wave crashes against the
shore, reaches a point on the beach and then recedes back
from where it came. That cresting point is a hinge moment, a
threshold moment from which events flow before cresting and
returning, before cresting and heading back down. Again, an
oversimplification, but that is the general idea behind chiastic
thought, an eastern thought pattern that is distinctly different
from western.

Bearing in mind that Jesus and his disciples were Jewish,
and that the land of Judea in Jesus' time was on the far eastern
end of the Roman Empire, it would be reasonable to deduce
that chiastic thought was, if not prevalent, certainly at least
present during the time of Jesus. Additionally, it would not
be unreasonable to say that the Bible is more accurately an
eastern document than western, so trying to approach the

20. Derived from the word *chiasmus,* which is a reversal in the order of
words in two otherwise parallel phrases, as in "He went to the country, to
the country went he."

Bible through a more eastern lens could provide new, more accurately reflective insight.

If you've ever driven in San Francisco, you know that common practice calls for, after parking on a street, turning your car's wheels away from the curb. Given the steep nature of the hills on which San Francisco is built, turning your wheels away from the curb serves as an extra precaution in the event that your emergency break fails. Instead of your car rolling uncontrollably down a hill, the tires will bump up against the curb and hold the car in place, thereby averting any accident or injury.

But let's suppose for a moment, that we park our imaginary car on a steep hill in San Francisco but fail to turn the wheels away from the curb. And let's further imagine that the emergency brake on our imaginary car fails, and the car slowly begins rolling down the hill, picking up speed as it goes.

As our car continues its descent (and since this is only imagination), let's say that a biker suddenly comes out of nowhere and is hit by our runaway vehicle, but that doesn't stop it! Instead, the car continues to careen down the hill toward (you've got to be kidding me!) a commuter bus filled with unsuspecting passengers whose driver, in a valiant, but ultimately unsuccessful attempt to swerve out of the way of our car, flips the bus over resulting in a tangled mess of steel and casualties! (Admittedly, my imagination can have a dark side at times!) And now, having narrowly avoided a head-on collision with the bus, our driverless car continues racing down the hill toward a gas station with a public service announcement poster that says, "Remember: when parking, turn your wheels away from the curb!"

And, because this is a story invented to prove a point, the irony is lost on us because—just as we finish reading the

PSA—our imaginary car slams into a gas pump, igniting the fuel and sending a giant fire cloud into the sky that can be seen and felt from miles away!

Being the responsible citizens that we are, we make our way down the hill as quickly as possible (it takes a while because there is, after all, a *lot* of carnage), past the hurt bicycle rider, past the debris field of the bus and its casualties, eventually arriving on scene at the fire-engulfed gas station to our car which is, inexplicably *not on fire!*

Even more amazing, after we climb into the car and put the key into the ignition, it starts and, as fortune would have it, right next door is a mechanic who promptly replaces the faulty emergency break without explaining the repair to us like we were two-years-old and then *not* overcharging us (this is make-believe, after all).

Problem fixed, right?

Though this story didn't need to be so drawn out and ridiculous, my point is that no one who is even slightly in touch with reality would believe that, by fixing the parking brake, everything is now all right with the world. Just fixing the cause of the problem would not be sufficient without seeking to make right the myriad of tragic consequences that the problem created. The fire at the gas station must be contained and then extinguished. The casualties from the crashed bus must be given first aid and transported to hospital. The biker must be located and treated. Sure, fix the emergency break—but that is not enough. Every effort must be made to try to restore all these things to the way they were before the brake failure.

During one of our trips to the Holy Land, our group had occasion to meet with a teacher of the Talmud whom we leaders had befriended on previous trips. The conversation was far-ranging in scope, but I particularly remember the teacher's discussion around the word and the concept of *shalom*. Typically, the word is translated as peace and, while accurate, falls far short of capturing the breadth and scope of Jewish understanding of the word. As described by this teacher of the Talmud, *shalom* not only means peace, but also the flourishing of all creation; it means men and women living rightly together, that the full created order of humans, animals, and plants exist in harmony with the Creator and humanity, shameless in the presence of God. Shalom is a peace that is complete, total, and all-encompassing. As the teacher of the Talmud explained, when a Jew says "Shalom" to someone, they are saying, "May it be for you as God always intended."

This begs the question: what had God always intended for his creation? Or perhaps a better question might be, in the Scriptures, where do we see the clearest picture of what God intended for his creation? Would it not be Genesis, chapters one and two, prior to the fall of humanity in chapter three?

When I taught Old and New Testament to college students, my premise was that Genesis, chapters one through eleven simply inform us of how things went awry for humanity. In Genesis chapter 12, we see God figuratively rolling up his sleeves and sharing what he is going to do about it. In other words, the rest of the Bible story is God at work, creating a holy people for himself. The rest of the Bible tells the story of God at work setting things right, restoring things to the way they were always intended to be. It is the story of God working to restore shalom.

To put this into a chiastic framework of thought, we know from whence we came, namely the Garden of Eden which we find in Genesis, chapters one and two. We also know to where we are heading—back to the way God always intended life to be, back to the beginning. In fact, our scriptures hint at this through the symbolism of the Tree of Life which appears, interestingly in only two books of the Bible: Genesis and Revelation.[21] Even more intriguing is that if one reads Genesis, chapters one and two, and then reads Revelation, chapters 21 and 22 (the first two and last two chapters of our Bible), one finds an unmistakable sentiment that is attempting to be conveyed. Both sections of scripture speak of an existence where all creation is flourishing, where men and women are once again living rightly together and the full created order of humans, animals, and plants are existing in harmony with the Creator. Both sections of scripture speak to an existence where, once again, humanity stands shameless in the presence of God in a peace that is complete, total, and all-encompassing.

What did God always intend? Shalom.

To what destination is God taking us? Shalom.

We are moving forward to the past. Within a chiastic framework of thought, we are moving from A (Genesis, chapters one and two), the way God always intended it to be, to A (Revelation, chapters 21 and 22), the way God always intended it to be. This being the case, then what is the hinge moment, the threshold event that would be represented by D in the simple formula of Eastern thought, ABCDCBA?

Before seeking an answer to that question, however, let us first come to understand how intimate the crucifixion of Jesus was.

IN A LAND THAT WAS LARGELY DESERT, WOOD WAS A RARE AND expensive commodity in first century Judea. Consequently, it was reserved for royalty and the wealthy (those who could afford to import it), but if it was needed for more mundane

---

21.   Genesis 2:9 & 3:22-24 and Revelation 2:7 and 22:2, 14 & 19

matters— crucifixions, for example—it was used sparingly and economically. For this reason, the Romans would locate a place outside of a city's wall where a few trees would then be identified (typically on a hill), stripped of their branches, leaving only bare trunks. Then cross beams would be fashioned that could be laid across the top of these trunks, forming a t-shape. These cross beams could be used over and over, requiring that no additional (and expensive) trees be utilized.

In most depictions of crucifixion, the image is of a large cross onto which a criminal is nailed, then lifted into position, high above the crowds so that those who are being crucified can be seen from a distance, serving as an example and visual deterrent (*The Passion*, by producer Mel Gibson comes immediately to mind). Following is picture of a woman who is 5'10" tall standing next to a tree trunk that has been fashioned to be used repeatedly for crucifixion.

What is your first thought or impression after seeing a *typical* crucifixion tree with a woman of average height standing next to it?

When I first encountered this, I was struck by the fact that the person being crucified was not elevated so high as to be out of reach of those observing. In fact, scripture says that,

> *"Jesus knew that his mission was now finished, and to fulfill Scripture he said, 'I am thirsty.' A jar of sour wine was sitting there, so they soaked a sponge in it, put it on a hyssop branch, and held it up to his lips." (John 19:28-29, NLT)*

The following picture is of a hyssop branch whose length averages only 1 ½ to 2 feet.

I don't know about you, but I always assumed that a hyssop branch was more along the lines of an oak or maple tree branch, a few feet long *because* I had an image of Jesus nailed to a cross and towering above the ground. Logically, but erroneously, I assumed that in order to reach high enough to get the sour-wine-soaked sponge to him, the hyssop branch had to be a few feet long! My point is that, contrary to the image we may have in our minds, the crucifixion was a highly personal and intimate event.

Jesus was *not* hoisted high above those observing, rather he was at practically eye level with them! This means that, if someone threw a rock at Jesus, it didn't miss.

If someone spit at him, it landed on Jesus.

If someone cursed Jesus, he heard it...every word.

He literally felt, beyond the nails, the jolting pain of a rock, the demeaning moisture of someone's spit and the mocking, condescending and hateful words being spoken to, and about him.

Because of the intimacy of a crucifixion, this also meant that if Jesus spoke, everyone around could hear! This is important to note because Jewish Rabbis regularly employed a teaching method designed to help jog the memory of students who had memorized the scriptures.

As an example, if you read the words, "A stitch in time..." you most likely know how to finish this most common of phrases. A stitch in time, saves nine."

If you read the words, "An apple a day...," you know that what follows is "...keeps the doctor away."

For the financially prudent, if you read the words, "A penny saved...," most likely your memory will be jogged to complete the phrase "... is a penny earned."

For those of us who grew up in the 70s and 80s: if I were to sing to you the words "Just sit right back and you'll hear a tale..." you might begin singing the rest of the introduction song to the popular television series, *Gilligan's Island*. And due to a relatively recent remake, if I began to sing to you the words "Here's the story, of a lovely lady, who was bringing up three very lovely girls…" many of you would begin singing the rest of the words to the theme song to the television series of the 70s, *The Brady Bunch*.

A more recent example might be if I sang to you the words: "So no one told you life was gonna be this way…" we would hear four quick hand claps, thanks to the hit television series of the 90s, *Friends*. Something you memorized long ago can be triggered back to full memory with the recitation of the first line, the first phrases and/or words. Why is this important to know?

Most devout Jews made it a course of discipline to memorize at least the Pentateuch, the first five books of the bible (Genesis, Exodus, Leviticus, Numbers and Deuteronomy). Beyond that, many memorized the Psalms and Proverbs on their way to memorizing the full text of what we call the Old Testament. *Memorized!* Think about that for a moment! Perhaps you have a "life verse" that you struggle to remember—or when needing to recite it, choose a rather loose paraphrase instead?

So, keeping in mind the intimate nature of the crucifixion, how close people were to Jesus, and the fact that most devout Jews had memorized scripture, then read this passage again:

> "At noon, darkness fell across the whole land until three o'clock. At about three o'clock, Jesus called out in a loud voice, 'Eli, Eli, lema sabachthani?' which means 'My God, my God, why have you abandoned me?'" (Matthew 27:45-45, NLT)

Jesus' last words are the first line of Psalm 22.

Could it be that, rather than crying out in a moment of despair, Jesus the Rabbi, being the quintessential teacher, is seeking to provide insight, is teaching with his last breaths? Could it be that Jesus was employing this common teaching technique, reciting the first line of the Psalm knowing that devout Jews would intuitively begin quietly reciting the memorized text?

Let's assume for a moment that this was, in fact, Jesus' intention. When one reads Psalm 22, there are uncanny similarities to what the Psalm says and what is unfolding at Jesus' crucifixion.

For example, as those standing near the cross are reciting the Psalm in their heads, they would reach this verse:

"'He trusts in the Lord,' they say, 'let the Lord rescue him. Let him deliver him, since he delights in him.'"
(Psalm 22:8, NLT)

Matthew's Gospel records:

"In the same way the chief priests, the teachers of the law and the elders mocked him, 'He saved others,' they said, 'but he can't save himself. He's the king of Israel!'" (Matthew 27:41-42a, NLT)

While continuing to recite the Psalm, they'd eventually reach this verse:

"Dogs surround me, a pack of villains encircles me; they pierce my hands and feet. All my bones are on

*display; people stare and gloat over me. They divide
my clothes among them and cast lots for my garment."
(Psalm 22:16-18, NLT)*

We find this description in Matthew's Gospel:

*"When they crucified him, they divided up his clothes
by casting lots." (Matthew 27:35, NLT)*

It is my contention that those who were present at Jesus'
crucifixion, those who were so close in proximity to him
hanging agonizingly on the cross and therefore able to hear
the words "My God, my God, why have you abandoned me;"
these devout Jews began reciting Psalm 22.

Furthermore, in doing so, there emerged among them
a general dawning that this Psalm was somehow coming
to life–was being played out before them in real time. Jesus,
the Rabbi, the teacher was still teaching them!

Even as his final breath approached, he was still struggling to help them understand what was transpiring. Even
as death loomed, Jesus chose to teach those who would
learn by reciting the first line of Psalm 22, knowing that its
familiarity would compel a recitation of the whole Psalm in
their minds. As would any good teacher, he was attempting
to lead those who were present to the objective of his lesson,
namely that what was transpiring before them—that experience in which they were personally participating—was
Psalm 22 in real time!

I suggest that *this* is the chiastic hinge moment, the
threshold moment or the "D" in the chiastic flow! Everything
thus far in the story of God has been flowing to *this* moment
on the cross and now, would begin to flow *out* from it!

From the way it was always intended to be in the beginning, to the falling away of creation, to the covenant with Abraham, to the kingdom of Israel to the exile; all were leading up to this moment, this defining, chiastic, hinge moment.

Jesus is trying to teach those present at the crucifixion and who were willing to still learn that this event, this tragically redemptive moment on the cross is *the* event that now turns the course of the story of God and begins the journey back to the beginning, back to the way it was intended to be.

Of the four gospels, John's was written the latest, sometime between 90-100AD of the common era. Consequently, John would have the benefit of a little more collective hindsight from which to draw, being written more than sixty years after Jesus' death and resurrection. Recounting the crucifixion, John records Jesus' final moments like this:

> *"Jesus knew that his mission was now finished, and to fulfill Scripture he said, 'I am thirsty.' A jar of sour wine was sitting there, so they soaked a sponge in it, put it on a hyssop branch, and held it up to his lips. When Jesus had tasted it, he said, 'It is finished!' Then he bowed his head and gave up his spirit." (John 19:28-20, NLT)*

"It is finished!"

What is finished?

Those of us with the benefit of more than two thousand years of hindsight know that the story was far from finished, that three days later Jesus would be resurrected. We know Jesus spent time with his disciples before ascending to heaven! We know of the initial call and ministry of the disciples and the spread of the Gospel, first to Jews and then Gentiles! We know the story continues with centuries of shining moments of the Christian church, with corresponding seasons of shame!

So, to what is Jesus referring when he says it is finished, because hindsight tells us that the story was far from finished (and even now, isn't finished yet)?

I suggest that Jesus was declaring that, with his death, the "D" in the chiastic flow, the chiastic hinge and threshold moment is what was finished. Jesus was teaching that this moment of his death and crucifixion was now finished, and with it, the peak of the roller coaster has been crossed and the wave has crested, so all things can begin flowing forward and back from whence they came! In other words, we have turned the proverbial corner and begun moving back to the way it was always intended to be, back to shalom, back to the garden.

We are moving forward to the past!

In fact, I don't believe it is a coincidence that the last book of the New Testament, *Revelation*, is also written by John and he adds this seemingly innocuous verse:

> *"And the one sitting on the throne said, 'Look, I am making everything new!' And then he said to me, 'Write this down, for what I tell you is trustworthy and true.'" (Revelation 21:5, NLT)*

What is being made new? Everything!

All creation is being restored, and the final two chapters of the *Book of Revelation* (Chapters 21 & 22) read like a variation on the first two chapters of the *Book of Genesis* giving a description of what a restored kingdom would look like. When Jesus says he is "...making everything new..." he is referring to shalom, the way it was intended to be.

He is re-creating, restoring, bringing back shalom by moving us forward to the past!

Jesus is not only bringing peace, but also the flourishing of all creation, men and women once again living rightly together.

He is making new the full created order of humans, animals, and plants so they can once again exist in harmony with their Creator, and humanity is being restored to shamelessness in the presence of God, enveloped in a peace that is complete, total, and all-encompassing!

Everything!

Everything is being made new!

"My God, my God, why have you abandoned me?"

These are not words of defeat, of someone despairingly calling out in their moment of abandonment. These are the words of *the Rabbi*, the quintessential teacher who, in his final moments utilized a common teaching technique and who, with his final breaths sought to convey—to any who would still listen and learn—what was truly transpiring in their very presence and in which they were unwittingly participating.

Unlike those who stood next to Jesus as he sought to teach them, we do not have an excuse to miss the magnitude of what he was seeking to convey We have the benefit of 20/20 hindsight and, as resurrection people can mature spiritually, learning to live with the paradoxes of faith.

Weakness and strength coexist as do light and darkness, despair and hope.

We know that in order to live, one must first die—and that as a resurrection people we paradoxically believe dead things can live again, that the old can be renewed and restored.

Perhaps most importantly, because of a horrific crucifix-ion ending in an empty tomb, we believe the world does *not* exist between the holy and the profane, but rather between the holy and the not-yet holy.

Why? Because this Rabbi, this Teacher said he is making everything new; *everything*!

We are moving forward to the past because God is at work making it as he always intended it to be.

In order to begin to grasp the implications of what this means for the way we understand, view and interact with the world today, we must decide if we are gardeners, or if we are only plant hospice care workers.

That is the focus of the next chapter.

CHAPTER 11

Walk to the Cross—Gardner Vs. Plant Hospice

(John 20)

W hen I was growing up, my father and mother maintained a vegetable garden and, while it meant that our family enjoyed fresh produce throughout the summer and fall, I spent a disproportionate amount of my childhood tending the garden (aka, pulling weeds, what today we would call, child labor). Consequently, I never experienced the many therapeutic elements about which so many speak when it comes to gardening (unless yanking things out of the ground in frustration and throwing them in a pile that I would later need to haul to the trash qualifies at therapeutic!).

So, it is no wonder that an aversion to gardening was one of the many things my future wife and I had in common when we first met. One might say the seeds of our love fell on the fertile soil of mutual disdain for gardening! In fact, the two of us have long since made our peace with the unique role we play in the life cycle of plants, particularly house plants. We recognize that there are those that sow seeds, give birth to, and lovingly cultivate healthy maturity in all sorts of plants. We call them Gardeners and admire them for their incredible touch and giftedness. Then there are those who assist plants at the end of their life, seeking to make their last days more comfortable. This is where we fit in the plant continuum of life, functioning more in the role of plant hospice care. More to the point, our home is where plants come to die, and we seek to provide them with as much comfort and dignity as possible.

Some of Jesus' most ministry defining moments were experienced in garden settings. One can easily imagine Jesus, the disciples, and others who joined along the way enjoying time together in the tranquil settings of various gardens. Paradoxically, it was in a garden that Jesus prayed, sweating drops of blood, asking if what lay ahead of him could pass him by (Luke 22:44), and was then betrayed by one of his so-called friends. A few days later, Jesus' body was interred in or near a garden, so it is not unreasonable to deduce that, for Mary and the disciples, gardens could symbolize a strange paradox of joy and peace alongside conflict and death. In Jesus, divinity and humanity resided; in a garden, peace and joy co-mingled with betrayal and death.

There is another place in scripture where divinity conflicted with humanity, where peace and joy co-mingled with betrayal and death, namely in Genesis, chapters 1 and 2, the Garden of Eden; that brief point in time when all creation existed as God intended it to be.

"Then God looked over all he made, and he saw that it was very good." (Genesis 1:31, NLT)

Introduced in a preceding chapter, the understanding of shalom is critical to a healthy faith identity. By way of reminder, even though most versions of the Bible translate *shalom* as peace, the actual meaning is much more encompassing and richer. Author Cornelius Plantinga Jr. in his book entitled *Not the Way It's Supposed to be: A Breviary of Sin* brings us closer to the full essence of the meaning when he writes that shalom is "...the webbing together of God, humans, and all creation in justice, fulfillment, and delight." He adds that shalom means "...universal flourishing, wholeness and delight–a rich state of affairs in which natural needs are satisfied and natural gifts fruitfully employed. Shalom, in other words, is the way things ought to be...the flourishing of human life in all aspects, as God intended it to be."[22]

Shalom means that all is flourishing, not only humanity, but ALL creation. It signifies men and women living rightly together, God and humanity living rightly together, living without fear and living without shame to the full potential, and for the full benefit of all creation. In short, shalom means "May it be as God always intended it to be."

The garden of Eden is an image, a symbol of what God intended creation to look like, and it would not be a stretch to state that this imagery simmers beneath the surface and psyche of any devout Jew, especially when standing within the tranquil, beautiful, innocent and peaceful setting of a garden.

So, when we join Mary in John 20, she is at the tomb of Jesus, weeping. The passage states that she looks into the tomb and sees...

---

22.   Plantinga, Jr., Cornelius, *Not the Way It's Supposed to Be: A Breviary of Sin*, Wm. B. Eerdman's Publishing Company, Grand Rapids, MI, 1995, pg. 10.

> *"...two white-robed angels, one sitting at the head
> and the other at the foot of the place where the body
> of Jesus had been lying. 'Dear woman, why are you
> crying?' the angels asked her. 'Because they have
> taken away my Lord,' she replied, 'and I don't know
> where they have put him.'" (John 20:12-13, NLT)*

I find Mary's casual demeanor toward two angels to be
noteworthy, almost as if she doesn't realize they are angels.
This is underscored by the fact that she doesn't even wait
for them to reply to her comment, because the next two
verses say...

> *"She turned to leave and saw someone standing there.
> It was Jesus, but she didn't recognize him. 'Dear
> woman, why are you crying?' Jesus asked her. 'Who
> are you looking for?' She thought he was the gardener.
> 'Sir,' she said, 'if you have taken him away, tell me
> where you have put him, and I will go and get him.'"
> (John 12:14-15, NLT)*

Irony begins to emerge as Mary doesn't recognize Jesus
either and instead assumes that, being in a garden, this
man must be the gardener. It might be interesting to recall
how John, the author of this Gospel, begins his testimony,
his account of Jesus Christ.

> *"In the beginning the Word already existed. The Word
> was with God and the Word was God. He existed
> in the beginning with God. God created every-
> thing through him, and nothing was created except
> through him. The Word gave life to everything that*

was created, and his life brought light to everyone."
(John1:1-4, NLT)

In other words, Mary fails to recognize the human embodiment of shalom, the embodiment of the way God intended it to be. Within the garden in which the tomb is found, Mary fails to recognize THE original gardener, fails to recognize that she is in a garden with God, the one who planted and cultivated all life into being! The many levels of symbolism are striking!

As the encounter continues, we learn that the man who Mary initially takes to be the gardener, reveals himself as (and/or she finally recognizes him as) Jesus, the Messiah. Then the reality of resurrection begins to dawn because, in John 20:18, Mary locates the disciples and informs them of what occurred. Here's where it begins to get good!

"That Sunday evening, the disciples were meeting behind locked doors because they were afraid of the Jewish leaders. Suddenly, Jesus was standing there among them! 'Shalom [Peace] be with you,' he said."
(John 20:19, NLT)

More accurately, Jesus said, "May it be with you as God—as I—always intended it to be." In other words, Jesus, the one who existed in the beginning and who gave life to everything created, Jesus' first word to his disciples upon his resurrection is "Shalom [Peace]," meaning "May it be with you like it was in the beginning, like it was in the Garden of Eden before the fall."

"As he spoke, he showed them the wounds in his hands

and his side. They were filled with joy when they saw
the Lord! Again he said, 'Shalom [Peace] be with you.
As the Father sent me, so I am sending you.'" (John
20:20-21, NLT)

It is during this new creation moment, when the grieving
disciples were wrestling with the reality that their beloved
Lord had been killed; when, from their frightened perspective, there now only seemed to be emptiness, chaos
and darkness, out of this void, life comes again—and
creation begins again! Jesus stands among them saying
"It will be as God always intended it to be. Shalom, the
created order will be restored." Then, as if to emphasize
this reality, he does something else uniquely reminiscent
of the story of creation.

"Then he breathed on them and said, 'Receive the holy
spirit.'" (John 22:22, NLT)

The image of God, breathing on a human, underscores
the relationship between the beginning and the present
moment.

"Then the Lord God formed the man from the dust
of the ground. He breathed the breath of life into the
man's nostrils, and the man became a living person."
(Genesis 2:7, NLT)

The parallels could not have been lost on the disciples. God
breathed and the man was given life. Jesus breathed and
the disciples received life by the Holy Spirit. God brought
creation into being. Jesus brings re-creation into being.

Joy and peace, conflict and death exist side-by-side in the Garden of Eden and in the garden tomb.

This is the essence of the holiest day in the church calendar: the celebration of Easter. The garden in which the risen Christ is interred represents the way God always intended it to be. It represents the state of shalom. Jesus is the embodiment of the way it was intended to be and is both the re-creator of the garden and the gardener that re-cultivates life. It is John who relates in his book of Revelation that Jesus, the quintessential gardener's ultimate purpose is this:

> *"And the one sitting on the throne said, 'Look, I am making everything new!' And he said to me, 'Write this down, for what I tell you is trustworthy and true.'"*
> *(Revelation 21:5, NLT)*

Jesus is making everything new! He is restoring the created order and returning it to the way it was always intended to be. He is *not* just saving the faithful but restoring it all! Not surprisingly, John also wrote:

> *"For God so loved the world: He gave his one and only Son, so that everyone who believes in him will not perish but have eternal life."* *(John 3:16, NIV)*

During the season of the church when we commemorate the resurrection of Jesus through our Easter celebrations, let's be clear about a few things *(I should warn those who grew up in a more legalistic perspective of biblical truth— these clarifications may be paradoxically liberating and terrifying).*

Let's be clear that we who claim to follow Jesus, those who love and pine for God are not simply waiting for this world to die, motivated by some twisted misguided idea that we will be whisked away to a better life; to a mythical location that is perfect. We do *not* view the world as a slow, dilapidating rental that we are just using. Such a perspective, while not only being unbiblical and against the intent of Christ (anti-Christ), encourages a deadly and dangerous indifference that contributes to the world's decay.

If Jesus is working to bring all creation back to the beginning; back to the way God always intended it to be, then the call to those of us who claim to follow Christ is not a posture of devout waiting and righteous suffering, but rather active partnership in cultivating and restoring the garden, recreating shalom whenever and wherever we can in this world, right here and right now! If Jesus is restoring all things to the way God intended it to be, then he is calling an army of gardeners, people who will fix, protect, cultivate, care for and love all creation, not people who specialize in plant hospice care, seeking to make the world more comfortable while awaiting its ultimate death.

In direct contrast to that old hymn's sentiment of "This world's not my home, I'm just passing through," we are not biding our time as the world fades away to nothing. In fact, the ultimate creator of life, the gardener of Eden declares that he is making all things new and restoring the created order to the way it was always intended to be. Those of us who claim to follow Jesus are to come alongside, endeavoring to cultivate, protect, grow and restore the world; the garden, to the state of being that was always intended.

I'm a firm believer that if you don't know where you're

going, any road will get you there, but where you end up, is most likely where you don't want to be. What we believe to be the intended result of Jesus' redemptive work dictates how we understand and engage the world in which we live. If we believe God's intent is that this world will ultimately end; will ultimately be destroyed and the "faithful" spared by being mystically whisked away, then at best, the result is an attitude of righteous judgementalism manifesting itself in indifference and apathy. At worst, it spiritualizes advocating for the earth's destruction in a twisted desire to hasten Jesus' return.

On the other hand, if we believe God's intent is the actual restoration of earth and ultimately the garden of Eden—the way God intended it to be; if we believe that the "faithful" are not going anywhere—then suddenly cultural and global issues take on a different urgency. How we engage and respond to global issues such as the facts of climate change, the disparity of wealth, the alarming rise of blended faith and patriotism (Christian nationalism), and the way the vulnerable, oppressed and refugee are viewed, received and cared for, become a matter of spiritual maturity. They become a matter of whether we are willing to join the work of restoration and recreation in which God is engaged through Jesus Christ. It becomes a matter of obedience.

It's hard to be indifferent and apathetic to something that is deeply and personally relevant. In fact, such a belief is sin. Jim Wallis, in his book *Christ in Crisis: Why We Need to Reclaim Jesus,* captures this as he writes "...when some people decide to have *dominion* over some other people, instead of stewardship *with* other people over the rest of creation, it literally is a sin against God's act of creation, and an overturning of God's original purposes in the world..."[23]

So how do we garden this world and cultivate shalom, thereby bringing the world closer to the way God intended it to be rather than lapse into the role of wringing our hands as we misguidedly await the word's demise? The answer is as broad in scope and depth as there are individual and collective people of faith, but the starting point is simultaneously easy to find and difficult to engage, because it starts from a posture of vulnerability.

About twenty years ago I read the book *Blue Like Jazz* by Donald Miller which included a few paragraphs in which he relates the story of a group of students setting up a confessional booth on Reed College campus during an annual end-of-year student festival called Renn Faire (short for "Renaissance Faire"). For perspective, picture a lot of college students, done with the pressures of a year filled with study and examinations, plenty of food, plenty of beverages to drink and an onsite clinic with staff who are specifically trained to assist students coming off bad trips. Against this backdrop, this group decided to set-up a confession booth, but with a very interesting and, I would suggest, biblical and Christ-like twist. As students entered the confession booth, instead of being invited to confess their sins, they instead were invited to hear the confessions of sins of the church on behalf of people of faith!

Author and public speaker Tony Kriz participated in this confessional booth and recounts his experience with the first fellow student that entered:

23. Wallis, Jim, Christ in Crisis: Why We Need to Reclaim Jesus, Harper One, 2019, pg. 46.

"'Welcome to the confession booth.' I [Tony Kriz] was having to remind myself to breathe between each sentence. 'This is where confessions are heard. If it is okay with you, I would like to begin.'

[The student] didn't move. He just stared at me. There was a slight tilt to his head. This was when it occurred to me that I didn't really know what I was going to say next.

'I am a Christian. Would you please forgive us?' I thought, that sounds weird, but I couldn't stop now. 'Would you please forgive us for the Crusades? Will you forgive us for the Inquisition?'

Suddenly my words took off with a life all their own, 'Would you forgive us for abusing kids placed under our care? Will you please, please forgive us for the role we played in slavery and racism in the US and around the world? Forgive us for wars waged in God's name? Will you forgive us for the ways we communicate judgment, arrogance and hatred every single day?' The words poured out.

My brain actually felt hot. My new friend just continued to stare. I think he was making space, allowing me to finish. I started to open my mouth again… 'Would you please forgive me?' For the first time I broke eye contact and lowered my eyes. 'Would you forgive me because I claim to be a follower of Jesus, but my life looks nothing like his? Jesus stood for love, generosity and care for others. Mine doesn't. I am selfish, distracted and dismissive all the time. Will you please forgive me?'

Until that moment, it had not occurred to me how much of a fraud I was. I walk around that beautiful campus claiming to be a representative of Jesus and yet...

Silence hung between us.

'Well,' he finally began, "that is the most f*ckingly beautiful thing I have ever heard in my entire life.'

I couldn't stop my smile. Plus, I didn't know f*ckingly was a word.

Then he did something that I had not prepared for... He forgave me.

His words were simple, 'I forgive you. I forgive you for all of it.' His voice was soft, and his eyes locked on mine. He did not cheapen the moment with excuses or justifications. He did not try to rescue me by telling me most of those things happened before I was even born. He did not play any of those games that are so commonplace in human exchange. He simply absolved me of my sin.

The power of words... the power of forgiveness is an intoxicating thing."[24]

This is one creative, wonderful and small example of someone seeking to move the world back toward what it was always intended to be, trying to nudge it back, closer to shalom. It reflects the posture that God assumed when,

---

24. Taken from the blog Tony Kriz, *Reed College...a Full Confession,* http://tonykriz.com/reed-college-a-full-confession/, 12/17/19

through the cries of a vulnerable infant later heard in the anguished cries of the crucified, a corner was turned in human history and we began our long, slow, and often painful journey back to the beginning. It is the faithful, emulating the vulnerability and servant heart of God that moves us forward to our past and the way things were always intended to be.

The original gardener, the one who planted and breathed life into all creation stands next to us, like he did with Mary. However, our despair, our fear, our anger, our self-righteousness blind us to the obvious. Our flawed understanding and erroneous theology of heaven blind us to the glaringly obvious biblical truth that Jesus—that God—wants us to love the world as he does. Jesus calls and expects us to join Him in restoring and tending to all creation as we seek to restore the garden through patient, loving cultivation.

Jesus is calling an army of gardeners, people who will fix, protect, cultivate, care for and love *all* creation, people who will love the world. He is not looking for those who are simply trying to make the world more comfortable while awaiting what they wrongly believe to be its ultimate death.

In fact, Jesus would be appalled by those of faith who, on some level, are secretly rooting for the demise of the world because it is in direct opposition to his ongoing work to restore, recreate shalom and bring *all* creation back to the way it was always intended to be.

Slowly read that last paragraph again and let the full implications of it sink in. If it makes you uncomfortable, then you certainly won't like what's next. Guess where the faithful are heading? To hell—with Jesus.

Read on.

CHAPTER 12

Jesus Wants Me to Go to Hell

(Matthew 16)

Jesus wants me to go to Hell.

Not that it is a common occurrence, but if someone tells me to go to hell, I have a very different response these days and it goes something like this: "I'm planning on it, because Jesus asked me to join him and I said 'yes.'" The look on peoples' faces is priceless and I confess that I get a perverse sense of joy from this—like when I blow in my dog's face. He's confused…but engaged.

I assure you that my response is biblical, gleaned from when Jesus said:

> *"And I tell you that you are Peter, and on this rock I will build my church, and the gates of hell will not overcome it." (Matthew 16:18, NIV)*

During biblical times, it was common for a city to be attacked and defended by vying powers because cities sat atop a source of water (quite necessary in a desert climate) and/or an important trade route. For example, the city of Megiddo has over twenty identifiable layers of destruction because its location was crucial to holding a trade route linking the known eastern and western lands. The political power that held the city of Megiddo was able to exert influence and control over trade which, unfortunately meant that the city changed hands numerous times. To put this in perspective, in a city as important as Megiddo it was not uncommon for a person to experience two or three sieges in their lifetime—at a time when life expectancy hovered around fifty years! Therefore, fortified cities with huge, defensible walls became the order of the day.

Obviously, gates were needed in the walls to allow regular access to the city when it wasn't being attacked, but these gates, while necessary for trade, were also the most vulnerable points in the city's defenses. Depending on the size of the city, there could be anywhere from two to eight gates ranging in height from 18 to 28 feet. Following are artist depictions of two of the main gates into Jerusalem, first the Golden Gate and then the Damascus Gate, side by side with how they appear today.

It is important to remember that there was no such thing as a master key that opened multiple gates. Each gate of a city had its own unique key and each key could be up to three feet in length (making the sale of tourist key chains impractical)! Since the gates were the most vulnerable part of a city's defense against enemies, the individual put in charge of the keys to the gates had to be highly trusted. If they failed to unlock the gates in the morning, commerce would be hindered and if they neglected to lock the gates at night, the city was vulnerable to attack. It is this vesting of responsibility and trust that is the origin of giving someone "the key to the city." In doing so, the city is saying that the recipient is deserving of, and is being given the collective trust of the city and its inhabitants.

An interesting side note: since these keys could be up to three feet in length and there could be, depending on the size of the city, anywhere between two and eight keys, one for each gate, the Key Keeper would typically throw the keys over his shoulder to transport them. From this practice, we get the idiom to "shoulder responsibility," conveying the idea that an individual accepts and assumes the responsibility for something. The individual to whom the keys of the city were entrusted, to a certain degree, was responsible for the rise and fall of their city. The kingdom, if you will, was in their hands.

The most vulnerable points of any defensive wall are the city gates, so a science developed around them, optimizing their effectiveness in an attack and minimizing their weaknesses. During times of peace, gates had several chambers through which the main road ran (see arrow below highlighting one of eight such chambers). These chambers were used for administrative purposes upon entry to the city, like paying taxes or registering. The picture below is of the remains of the Gates of Hazor—a city just north of the Sea of Galilee and destroyed by Joshua[25]—and may help conceptualize the administrative chambers on either side of the road into the city.

Between each set of chambers was a mini-gate and the chambers were enclosed with a hole in the roof leading to the main wall defenses that surrounded the city. With this design, an attacking army would not only have to breach the main city gate, but also each of the mini gates within. Defending soldiers could replace those who had been killed by dropping through the roof of the chambers and, in this way, continue to outnumber the attackers.

Exterior ramps to the gates were designed so that, if you were facing the gate, they sloped to the right down

25. Joshua 11:10-13.

along the wall, thereby rendering attackers more vulnerable. The overwhelming majority of people are right-handed, so soldiers would carry their shields on their left arm so that their dominant arm could wield their weapon. However, in order to advance up a ramp to the gate, attackers would have to turn in such a way so that their shield was closest to the city wall from which rocks were being thrown and arrows shot. This meant that they had to turn their bodies almost 180 degrees and back their way up the ramp in order to keep their shield in the most optimum defensive position, slowing their advance and making them more vulnerable.

What would it mean if a gate "prevailed" during a battle?

It would mean that the gate did its job, keeping the attackers out. When a gate prevails; when a gate "wins," those that were attacking are repulsed and the city remains in the hands of the defenders. In fact, throughout documents of antiquity phrases are found stating that "...the gates prevailed..." when the city was able to withstand the attack of the aggressors or outlast a siege. The point that needs to be understood is that, when a gate prevails, those on the attack are turned back.

Set this insight aside for the moment and we will come back to it.

ONE OF THE MOST CRITICAL MOMENTS FOR THE DISciples occurs in Matthew 16 when Jesus poses this question to them: "Who do you say I am?" *Where* Jesus most likely posed this question is as significant as how Jesus responded. Luke 8 provides us with a little more context because the events recorded there take place in the same proximity and general timeframe as the event in Matthew 16.

Within the culture of biblical times, water paradoxically symbolized not only chaos and death, but life as well. In the opening chapter of Genesis, the scriptures relate that…

"The earth was formless and empty, and darkness covered the deep waters. And the Spirit of God was hovering over the surface of the waters." (Genesis 1:2, NLT)

One gets the image of emptiness, swirling dark waters of chaos into which no one would want to fall. For this reason, the idea that evil spirits (and even a mythical sea monster) dwelled in water as evidenced in the scriptures (Psalm 74:13-14). On the one hand, water symbolizes chaos and death—and in Genesis, God hovers over death and chaos. Then, scripture says that God speaks, and order comes from chaos. With God's spoken word, the waters calm. Created order begins to emerge.

Given the cultural context and the fact that not all the disciples who followed Jesus were fishermen and comfortable on water, imagine how it was received when Jesus one day…

"…said to his disciples, 'Let's cross to the other side of the lake.' So they got into a boat and started out. As they sailed across, Jesus settled down for a nap. But soon a fierce storm came down on the lake. The boat was filling with water, and they were in real danger." (Luke 8:22-23, NLT)

The Sea of Galilee is a large fresh-water lake that is about thirteen miles long and eight miles wide (64 square miles).

Located near the Mediterranean Sea that encompasses 965,300 square miles, the Sea of Galilee is not all that big, and we can agree that calling it a sea is a generous designation. So, just how fierce would a storm be on this little lake, a storm so fierce that those who found themselves on a boat with Jesus would feel they were "...in real danger?"

I have personally witnessed how, in less than ten minutes, the surface of the Sea of Galilee transformed from calm and tranquil glass to waves that were easily four to five feet high! These violent storms are caused by the situation of the lake in the Jordan Rift with steep hills on all sides. The cooler air masses from the surrounding mountains collide with the warm air in the lake's basin. Winds sometimes funnel through the east-west-oriented valleys in the Galilean hill country and rush down the western hillsides of the lake. The most violent storms, however, are caused by the fierce winds which blow off the Golan Heights from the east. To give this perspective, the remains of a first century boat was discovered by accident in the winter of 1986 after a dry season when the lake was very low. It was found on the muddy shores of the Sea of Galilee near Magdala, and scholars agree that it may have functioned as a ferry or was used by fishermen. The remains of the boat are about 29 feet long and eight feet wide, so a similar boat could have transported Jesus and his disciples (even with Jesus stretched out and napping).

Following is a photograph of the first century boat, and next to it, a replica of how the boat could have appeared in its prime:

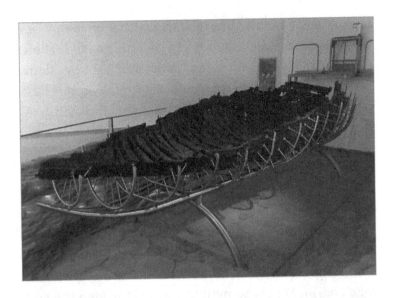

There's little doubt that with Jesus and his twelve disciples all in the boat, it would have been crowded; however, such a boat *would* have had the capacity to transport thirteen men. However, a more important question needs to be considered as it relates to the passage in Luke 8. If thirteen men got on board this first century boat, wouldn't their combined weight raise the water line, impacting the boat's vulnerability to waves? If the waterline on a boat is high and the boat is suddenly being hit by four to five-foot waves, there is a very real chance that such a boat could take on enough water to sink!

Keeping that in mind, this event from Luke takes on fresh meaning:

> *"So they got into a boat and started out. As they sailed across, Jesus settled down for a nap. But soon a fierce storm came down on the lake. The boat was filling with water, and they were in real danger. The disciples went and woke him up, shouting, 'Master, Master, we're going to drown!' When Jesus woke up, he rebuked the wind and the raging waves. Suddenly the storm stopped and all was calm. Then he asked them, 'Where is your faith?' The disciples were terrified and amazed. 'Who is this man?' they asked each other. 'When he gives a command, even the wind and waves obey him!'"* (Luke 8:23-25, NLT)

Remember, there is only one other time in scripture when the waters of chaos prevailed until a word was spoken and order came from chaos. Only one other time in scripture do the waters calm at the spoken word, and order begins to emerge. Of course, the disciples were amazed and terrified because they had just watched Jesus do what only God himself possessed the power to do: speak calm and order out of death and chaos!

Following Jesus' calming of the storm, the disciples regain control of the boat and realize that Jesus is sailing them to "… the region of the Gerasenes, across the lake from Galilee (Luke

8:26, NLT)." This region was known as the Decapolis, and the Greek roots of the name are indicative of the fact that the area was known as a non-Jewish, pagan stronghold. For all intents and purposes, the disciples' day went from bad to worse. After almost being swallowed up in the death and chaos of a storm, they are instructed to go to the very region that, for the devout Jew, symbolized and embodied absolute evil. The region of the Decapolis was the antithesis of godliness.

Then, just when the disciples thought it couldn't get any worse, guess who meets them as they arrive?

> *"As Jesus was climbing out of the boat, a man who was possessed by demons came out to meet him. For a long time he had been homeless and naked, living in the tombs outside of the town." (Luke 8:27, NLT)*

The disciples are met by the very definition of unclean: a naked man possessed by demons who lives among the dead, the proverbial winner of the trifecta of uncleanliness!

(But wait! There's more!)

> *"As soon as he saw Jesus, he shrieked and fell down in front of him. Then he screamed, 'Why are you interfering with me, Jesus, Son of the Most High God? Please, I beg you, don't torture me!' For Jesus had already commanded the evil spirit to come out of him. This spirit had often taken control of the man. Even when he was placed under guard and put in chains and shackles, he simply broke them and rushed out into the wilderness, completely under the demon's power.*
>
> *Jesus demanded, 'What is your name?'*

'Legion,' he replied, for he was filled with many demons. The demons kept begging Jesus not to send them into the bottomless pit.

There happened to be a large herd of pigs feeding on the hillside nearby, and the demons begged him to let them enter into the pigs. So Jesus gave them permission. Then the demons came out of the man and entered the pigs, and the entire herd plunged down the steep hillside into the lake and drowned." (Luke 8:27-33, NLT)

The naked and possessed man who lived among the dead had his demons cast out into a herd of pigs; animals that are considered unclean (Leviticus 11:27). Then these unclean, demon-possessed pigs ran down a steep hill and, in a frenzy of chaos and death, drowned themselves in the water!

As a former public, school principal, I must applaud Jesus on what is the definition of an effective field trip!

After the man was cleansed from the demons, Luke goes on to recount:

"The man who had been freed from the demons begged to go with him. But Jesus sent him home, saying, 'No, go back to your family, and tell them everything God has done for you.' So he went all through the town proclaiming the great things Jesus had done for him." (Luke 8:38-39, NLT)

As an interesting aside, non-biblical sources indicate that during this time period there was a surge of synagogues in this pagan region. While it is impossible to say that there is a direct correlation, it is interesting to speculate.

Around the same time frame, and with that field trip fresh in their minds, Matthew 16:13 indicates that Jesus and his disciples came to the region of Caesarea Philippi, about 25 miles north of the Sea of Galilee. During the time of Jesus, it was considered the center of a pagan fertility cult and home to the god Pan, the god of the flocks and fields.

There are indications that the location may have been a cultic center as early as the time of Joshua (Joshua 13:4-5 and Judges 3:3) and would likely have been a place where Baal was worshiped. Later in 1 Kings 12:25ff, King Jeroboam sets up some golden calves in this general vicinity, ultimately promoting the worship of Baal. The historical connection associated with this place of pagan worship would not have been lost on the devout Jew in Jesus' time. The cultic center stood on the side of a mountain and, from a cave flowed a spring that, even to this day, serves as one of the major contributories to the Jordan River. Below is a picture of the cave today as well as an artist rendition of how the cultic center may have appeared during Jesus' time.

It would not be an overstatement to say that, symbolically, the place where the manifestation of Baal was being worshipped during Jesus' time, a place where water (chaos and death) flowed from the entrance of a cave, was viewed as nothing short of the entrance to the underworld, what the Old Testament calls She'ol, or the pit. In other words, to the devout Jewish mind of the time, this was arguably the gate of hell itself.

To summarize: after a recent field trip with the disciples that included almost dying during a storm; a storm that Jesus calmed by speaking order from chaos—akin to God speaking to the void in Genesis—a visit to the pagan stronghold of the Decapolis where they met a naked, possessed man who lived among the dead, then observing the casting out of demons into a herd of unclean pigs, Jesus tops off the week with a quick stop at the symbolic entrance to hell itself.

Here, the book of Matthew records that, when...

> "...Jesus came to the region of Caesarea Philippi, he asked his disciples, 'Who do people say that the Son of Man is?' (Matthew 16:13, NIV)

While standing in front of the symbolic gate of hell, Jesus decides to ask what his disciples felt people were saying and thinking about who he is. Notice the breadth of answer they give:

> 'Well,' they replied, 'some say John the Baptist, some say Elijah, and others say Jeremiah or one of the other prophets.' (Matthew 16:14, NIV)

Then in "typical Jesus fashion," he bores down from the theoretical and speculative to the personal, asking the question of individual belief, faith and conviction.

> Then he asked them, 'But who do you say I am?' (Matthew 16:15, NIV)

Not surprisingly, Peter is the first to leap and make a personal declaration.

> *Simon Peter answered, 'You are the Messiah, the Son of the living God.' (Matthew 16:16, NIV)*

Note Jesus' answer, but as you do, remember what we learned about keys and gates. Remember as well that the disciples are standing in front of the symbolic gate of hell itself, She'ol:

> *Jesus replied, 'You are blessed, Simon son of John, because my Father in heaven has revealed this to you. You did not learn this from any human being. Now I say to you that you are Peter (which means 'rock'), and upon this rock I will build my church, and all **the gates of hell will not conquer it**. And I will **give you the keys of the Kingdom of Heaven**. Whatever you forbid on earth will be forbidden in heaven, and whatever you permit on earth will be permitted in heaven.'" (Matthew 16:13-19, NIV, emphasis added)*

For our Catholic brothers and sisters, this passage institutes the papal line that they have sought to meticulously maintain from Peter to the present-day Pope. For Protestants, this is the formal establishment of the church as the gathered followers of Jesus Christ. This latter tradition holds that the church is built upon Peter's confession of faith and his acknowledgement of Jesus as Messiah; therefore, all are part of the established church—what Evangelicals (including my chosen denomination, the Evangelical Covenant Church) refer to as "the priesthood of all believers."

It is interesting that in Matthew 16:19 Jesus states he is going to give Peter—and by extension, the church, the "...keys of the Kingdom of Heaven." Remember that the gates were the most vulnerable part of a city's defensive wall against enemies, so whoever oversaw the keys was trusted with immense responsibility! If he were to fail to lock the gates at night, he would leave the city vulnerable to attack. Whomever was entrusted with these keys was, to a certain degree, responsible for the rise and fall of their city! The kingdom, if you will, was in his hands.

More importantly however, is what Jesus says in Matthew 16:18b, that "...the gates of hell will not conquer it [the church]." Don't miss this subtle, but important nuance! I have heard over a dozen sermons on this passage, and all of them have conveyed in some way the idea that evil from hell itself is attacking the church from all sides, but the church will be safe behind these strong walls. The gates were, after all, being defended by God, by Jesus!

Remember! What would it mean if a gate prevailed during a battle?

It means that those who were attacking the gates of a city, did not get in! It means that those who were on the attack were turned back because the gates prevailed. It means that the gates did not crumble and did what they were designed to do" keep the attackers *out*!

So, while standing in front of the symbolic gate of hell itself, Jesus says...

"...and the gates of hell will not conquer it." (Matthew 16:18b, NIV)

Do you see it? Do you see who is attacking?

It is the *church* that is attacking the gates of hell and whatever those gates are protecting!

Do you see what Jesus is saying?

The gates of hell will not prevail and keep the church out! The gates of hell will not prevail against the attacking church!

Jesus, and those who choose to follow him, are going to hell! They are going to hell and and taking over.

So, if you tell me to go to hell, I will answer "I'm planning on it, because Jesus asked me to join him and I said 'yes!'"

Jesus did *not* run and hide from the world and the disciples did *not* cower behind some ill-conceived idea of walls while Jesus beat back evil. In fact, the imagery of this passage is the exact opposite. Jesus is leading his followers; he is leading the church forward against the gates that are protecting hell itself and...guess what? *Those gates are not going to prevail!* They are going to crumble!

In other words, Jesus and those following him will breach the gates protecting hell itself, enter in and expand the kingdom of heaven there as well![26]

One of the most beautiful Jewish theological tenants is that the world is not divided between the holy and profane, a common theological position held by most Protestant denominations, including my own. I categorically reject this idea and believe, along with my Jewish brothers and sisters, that the world is divided between the holy and the not-yet holy. Our call as God's people is to do all that we

---

26. Given the sad, misguided nature of current American politics and faith, I feel it is necessary to be careful and clear about something. The church is *not* on the attack militaristically, but rather by way of engaging the world and culture as Jesus engaged them.

can to make the world more holy and be more reflective of what it was always intended to be from the beginning. Our call is not to discern who is "in" and "out" of the kingdom of heaven, and then minimize our interaction with those we deem to be "out!"

Our call as humans, as the one and only being in all creation that uniquely "...bears God's image..." (Genesis 2), is to forge relationships with *all* people, not just those who are like us. Our call is to exist in those areas of the world that the righteously religious may deem evil or unclean and in so doing, bring holiness, *not* derision, disdain and judgement to the not-yet holy.

And while theologians will most assuredly disagree, when Jesus gives the Church the keys of the Kingdom of Heaven, I believe our responsibility moves beyond simply a confessed belief in Jesus Christ as our personal Lord and Savior. Let me be absolutely clear on this point. It is **not** enough to have a personal relationship with Jesus Christ if it doesn't motivate us to tend to God's creation as well. We shirk our responsibilities as keepers of the keys if we do not do all that we can to enhance the very kingdom that the gates are protecting.

OUR PERSONAL RELATIONSHIP WITH JESUS CHRIST IS meaningless if it doesn't motivate us to change systems and institutions that demean, degrade, and/or systematize the exploitation of people who bear God's image or destroy the created world that gives witness to the Creator.

Our personal relationship with Jesus Christ is meaningless if it is complicit in its silence while a segment of the faith dangerously combines faith and patriotism, dehumanizes certain ethnicities, is misogynistic, subverts care for the poor, refugee and destitute in the name of country over faith; or allows and affirms individual and collective treasure to benefit the most wealthy at the expense of the most vulnerable, especially when our investment portfolios are performing well.

Our personal relationship with Jesus Christ is meaningless if it in any way seeks to define who is excluded (versus included), if it is concerned with justifying theology based on investment portfolio performance at the expense of basic human decency.

Or, as writer, pastor and activist John Pavolvitz writes:

"...I see countless proudly unloving people claiming to be Christians, and it's baffling.

If you profess to be a follower of Jesus, I'm not concerned with your politics and I don't care about your doctrine. I'm not interested in the Scriptures you can recite or the prayers you utter out loud. Show me a working theology of empathy. Show me that you actually give a damn about people: not just Republican people or American people or Christian people or white people—but the disparate parade of human beings in every way you encounter them, in every condition they arrive, with whatever backstory they've lived through.

If you tell me you're a Christian, be someone who, like Jesus—looks at the crowds and has a compassion for them that propels them into proximity with their pain.

Because if you aren't deeply burdened to live from

a place of expansive, sacrificial, selfless love toward your neighbor, not moved to alleviate anguish or reduce suffering, not compelled to leave people better than you found them—honestly I'm not sure what the point is in calling yourself a Christian."[27]

I know this is a lot to digest and you may even be muttering under your breath, "Todd, you're crazy. Go to hell!"

I am, and I hope you'll join me.

---

27. Pavolitz, John. "Christians Are Supposed to Care About People." *Stuff That Needs to Be Said*. January 6, 2020, <u>Link to post.</u>

CHAPTER 13

Choose Me, Drunk Guy!

I found myself part of an impromptu social experiment the other day while riding a free shuttle bus between the conference center where I was attending a training session and my hotel. It was about 8:30pm and, after stepping aboard the bus, I worked my way to the back, since one of my favorite past times is people-watching, and everyone knows that the back seat is the best vantage point!

Since the shuttle's route took us through the downtown core, the fifteen or so passengers included a mixture of conference attendees, business folks that were obviously finishing a long day, and a tourist or two. We were at the second stop of twelve when a passenger came aboard who was obviously, as my grandmother would say, a "Weeble" (since he wobbled, but never fell down).[28] Grasping the first pole as the door closed behind him, almost lending a dramatic effect to his entrance, the gentleman looked down and tried to make eye contact with the two people sitting in the first seat who were, from what I could determine, working equally as hard to avoid eye contact.

As the bus pulled away toward its next stop, this newest rider pointed at the young man on the aisle and declared

---

28. Google "What is a weeble?" for context. You're welcome.

in a loud enough voice so that all could hear (but not in a threatening manner), "You're in!" Then he pointed at the older gentleman sitting by the window and stated "You're in too!" With that, he reached for the next pole, wobbled (but didn't fall) and grabbed hold of it, bringing him in line with the next set of seats and three other passengers, whose careful efforts to avoid eye contact made the first two passengers look like they weren't even trying!

He looked left, then right before pointing at a middle-aged woman in a smart business suit. With a tinge of sadness he said, "You're not in." Then he turned his gaze to her seat mate, a younger woman who appeared to be coming from an exercise class and, in a surprise-announcement accompanied by a slight smile, he said, "But you're in!" Then turning to an older gentleman seated across the aisle, his conference badge hanging outside his shirt, top button undone and loosened tie, the Weeble announced, "You're not in."

As he reached for the next pole and began maneuvering to the next set of seats, you could sense people beginning to relax a bit as they realized that, while a bit off-putting, this Weeble wasn't dangerous. Only one person was occupying the next row of seats, an elderly woman to whom he pointed and declared, "You're in." The woman graciously smiled and said, "Thank you." This pleased the Weeble and he reached for the next pole, almost missing his hold as the bus lurched slightly. But in a surprising display of agility—and despite his liquid-induced joyful disposition—he grabbed the next pole and managed to stabilize himself.

At this point, my perch for people-watching really paid off because, from my vantage point at the back of the bus, I could see the remaining handful of passengers seated in

front of me. Astonishingly, I noticed most of them beginning to sit a little straighter in their seats and, even though
two of the three in the next row were declared "not in," all
of them made eye contact and smiled, awaiting the verdict.
One gentleman even straightened his tie just before the
Weeble arrived at his row and, thankfully, his effort was
rewarded, smiling sheepishly after being declared "in."

So, what exactly was the definition of "in?" None of
us had any idea, but clearly whatever club this inebriated
individual was creating, everyone on board wanted an all-
access pass!

I watched him declare three more people "in" and two
unfortunate people "not in," before he finally reached my
seat, the last one on the bus. In retrospect, this was one of
those comical, surreal moments when it seemed that time
slowed down. I stole a glance past the Weeble and noted
that most of the passengers had turned in their seats to
watch—because who'd want to miss the final moment? (That
would be like watching the Masked Singer every week but
turning off the television just as they are about to take off
their mask! Who would do that?)

Just as the man was about to declare my fate, I held up
my hand and said "Wait!"

My voice surprised both him and the other passengers,
because apparently, I had violated some rule of which everyone else but me was aware. But I was committed! I was all
in, and there would be no turning back. Those who know
me will be surprised by what I said next and, quite honestly,
I surprised myself because this response is not typical of me.
Capitalizing on the brief opening afforded by the moment,
I said, "I already know I'm 'in' and, I checked with God and
he told me everyone on the bus is 'in' too!"

A lot happened in the next three or four seconds, even though it felt like a full minute or two. I had a mental image of an old Western movie, when the camera zeros in on the eyes of each gunfighter as the whole town watches and waits, holding their collective breath. (I am nearly convinced that the theme music from "The Good, the Bad, and the Ugly" was playing in the background.)

The man and I watched one another for a tell, a slight movement, a giveaway that would indicate what was to happen next. Almost imperceptibly at first, I saw the corners of his eyes begin to smile and then, he took a step back, let out a laugh and proclaimed, "You're right!"

Then, in what still feels like a surreal moment, the passengers began to clap and cheer at the surprise ending. It was an "Oprah moment" as everyone realized they would be getting off at their stops with their own memberships to the still-undetermined club of the drunk guy on the shuttle bus!

EVERY PERSON HAS A DEEP, DEEP NEED TO BE PART OF something, to be included. Paradoxically we also carry an unarticulated sense of dread that we may end up alone, forgotten and lonely, that we may one day find ourselves strangely apart from others. Regardless of the complexities, biases, difficulties and pain that come from being in relationship, especially with those who are not like us, no one wants to be left out—even if it means silently calling out "Choose me, drunk guy!" to be allowed into whatever group he is forming on this evening shuttle bus of strangers heading home after a long day.

The God we serve, the Christ we follow, the Spirit to which we seek to yield works toward one thing: *to restore shalom and make the world once again the way God always intended it to be.*

Anything less, is working against God and against Christ. Or to phrase it more directly, anything less is anti-God, anti-Christ and anti-restoration through complicity, or worse.

Every one of the stories, lessons and sermons I have shared have a common theme. Once we understand a small nuance, one that the Bible assumes we know, then familiar and comfortable passages take on new, and initially uncomfortable meaning and application.

These nuances consistently reveal a *God who will go infinitely further than we would ever dream or imagine when restoring relationship on the way to restoring shalom.*

If your faith or your faith community, overtly or subtly, seeks to define who is "out" versus starting with the assumption that all are "in," you are working against shalom, the way God intended it to be.

If your faith or faith community, overtly or subtly, operates from a paradigm that inextricably blends the vitality of one's faith with patriotism for one's country, you are working against shalom, the way God intended it to be.

If your faith or faith community, overtly or subtly, cites the authority of scripture but minimizes those passages that make painful demands, while simultaneously elevating those passages that console and assuage our feelings, you are working against shalom, the way God intended it to be.

If your faith or faith community, overtly or subtly, sees and paints the world as innately bad and evil, while simultaneously highlighting the faithful's "temporary status," assuring them they will be whisked away at a future, appointed time, you are working against shalom, the way God intended it to be.

If your faith or faith community, overtly or subtly, gives you permission to ignore by silence those proclaimed brothers and sisters who demean, degrade, mock, belittle, bully, gaslight and/or justify any action or deed, individual or collective, that is contrary to the heart, compassion, spirit and dignity extended to all by Jesus Christ, you are working against shalom, the way God intended it to be.

If your faith or faith community, overtly or subtly, sees certain statements of the Bible as permanent injunctions for all time, but sees Jesus' command to love enemies, care for the poor, welcome the refugee or view the Sermon on the Mount as being so strangely full of nuance that it never seems to apply to you, you are working against shalom, the way God intended it to be.

If your faith or faith community, overtly or subtly, remains silent as segments of people are vilified or dehumanized, ignores and therefore condones misogyny, looks away when one race declares their superiority over another and invokes the Bible or God as justification, you are working against shalom, the way God intended it to be.

Lest I be accused of casting a stone, let me be clear: the uncomfortable perspectives I've shared here come from the uncomfortable awareness that I am the one who calls out "Choose me, drunk guy!" because, more often than not, I am more fearful of being apart from people and popularity than apart from the presence of God.

The truth of these words is deeply personal because they rip back the curtain of unwanted self-awareness to reveal that I am Israel, because I struggle with God every minute of every day.

They come from the uncomfortable and unwanted self-awareness that I am the one whose first impulse is to remain quiet when I see wrong being committed.

They come from the uncomfortable and unwanted self-awareness that I am also the one who, out of desperation, grabs for the tassels of Jesus' hem.

They come from the uncomfortable and unwanted self-awareness that I am the one who betrays the relationship even as God is working to restore it.

They come from the uncomfortable and unwanted self-awareness that I, with tearful fear and shame, look up into the face and eyes of Jesus who, out of abundant mercy, grace, and love, moves shalom a glacial step closer to me by saying, "Then neither do I condemn you."

They come from the uncomfortable and unwanted self-awareness that the God we serve, the Christ we follow, the Spirit to which we seek to yield seeks one thing: to restore shalom and make it, once again, the way God always intended it to be.

They come from the uncomfortable and unwanted self-awareness that, if I am to truly reflect the heart of Jesus and serve the most vulnerable and poor, then I must give up trying to hold cultural power through politics and accept that, in pursuit of a deepening relationship with Jesus, it may cost me more than I imagined—and I may even feel taken advantage of.

THOUGH I DON'T GARDEN, I AM SURE OF THIS: THOSE who do, get dirty, sore, and wonder if it's all worth it. But then, they remember what the garden will look like when it is in full, healthy bloom, and they bend low to pick another weed, rake another row, and till the soil as sweat drips from their brow.

We know what the garden looks like, and we know that God is working to restore this garden to the way it was always intended to be.

So, let's get dirty. Let's get sore muscles, tired feet, and at times wonder if it's all worth it.

Because even as we wonder, we already know that it is—it is all worth it.

So, let's continue the work, shall we?

Shalom.